THE GENTLE WAY II

A SELF-HELP GUIDE FOR THOSE WHO BELIEVE IN ANGELS

BENEVOLENT OUTCOMES: THE STORY CONTINUES

TOM T. MOORE

THE GENTLE WAY II

A SELF-HELP GUIDE FOR THOSE WHO BELIEVE IN ANGELS

BENEVOLENT OUTCOMES: THE STORY CONTINUES

TOM T. MOORE

 Light Technology Publishing

Cover Artist:
Walter Bruneel
www.iasos.com

ISBN-10: 1-891824-80-5
ISBN-13: 978-1-891824-80-7

Published by:

Technology
PUBLISHING

PO Box 3540
Flagstaff, AZ 86003
928-526-1345

www.LightTechnology.com

DEDICATION

This book, *The Gentle Way II*, is dedicated to all of the people who shared their stories with me.

In memory of Joy Hart-Boese, a good friend.

TABLE OF CONTENTS

FOREWORD

Since my first book was released in 2006, many, many events have occurred in my life, including one life-threatening event that you'll read about later in this book. In November of 2007, I decided to begin a monthly newsletter mostly filled with the emails I kept receiving from readers of the articles I was writing for *Sedona Journal of Emergence!* and some regional magazines. I thought I might be able to gather enough material for a once-a-month letter. Well, this quickly became biweekly and then weekly as people sent my newsletter to their friends, and their friends forwarded it on to their friends. It really took on a life of its own as more and more people emailed me with their success stories of requesting most benevolent outcomes (MBOs)[1] and living prayers, as I called them in my first book (in this book they are referred to as "benevolent prayers." I began using the phrase "I ask any and

---

[1] The words "benevolent outcome," "most benevolent outcome" and the abbreviation "MBO" are used interchangeably throughout this book. These terms all mean and refer to the same thing.

all beings . . ." more and more when I said a benevolent prayer. I found that it was much easier to remember, and it seemed to fit well with the phrase "I request a most benevolent outcome . . ." that I used when I was requesting something specifically for myself (you use the phrase "I ask . . ." when you are requesting something for someone other than yourself).

I must also thank all of you who have contributed your success stories and questions. Many readers have expressed a desire to have sort of a reference guide that they can refer to when specific situations arise. Therefore, this book is divided into chapters by subject, according to reader wishes. If you've purchased multiple copies of my first book to give to friends and family, let them know about this new book. Please be aware that I did have to condense some of the letters that were sent to me, and some were corrected for grammatical and typographical errors. Some names have been changed as well, usually at the request of the letter-writer.

My guardian angel tells me this simple, yet powerful spiritual tool will still be in use hundreds of years from now, as it's the best way you and everyone else can keep on your life paths. So have fun reading these many inspiring stories from people all over the planet. You'll find that they are more similar than different to you. I think that this is another reason why I was suppose to be doing all this work—to bring you all together. Expect great things!

A LITTLE REVIEW

After my first book, *The Gentle Way*, was published, I began to receive a number of emails from all over the world each month from people who'd been requesting benevolent outcomes, some asking about what to request in specific instances. For those of you who are reading for the first time about requesting most benevolent outcomes (MBOs), these are specific requests that you say when you desire assistance from your guardian angel. Your guardian angel will help you with even the most mundane requests, such as requesting a parking space near a busy restaurant or store. As an example, recently my wife and I went to a press screening of a new motion picture. The screening was taking place at a theater located in a busy shopping center. I said, "I request a most benevolent outcome for a parking place near the mall entrance. Thank you!" When we arrived at the theater, there was my parking space, waiting for me at the end of the row nearest the mall entrance. I recommend starting with these simple requests, so you can get immediate feedback that these requests work. A quick note on requesting MBOs: Always thank your guardian angel, and say it with some emotion.

When you begin to trust in the effectiveness of MBOs, then you can use them for more important things. My wife and I decided we wanted to downsize our home, as both our children are adults now. My wife kept dragging me to see one house after another during the middle of the workday. I started requesting a benevolent outcome to buy each house, as I knew my guardian angel would not let me buy the wrong house after an MBO request. We even made an offer on one— and then someone paid the full asking price, which is almost unheard of in these down-market times. Finally I said: "I request a most benevolent outcome for the perfect house for us. Thank you!" The next day she found our house, and we were able to buy it at a great price, as the family selling it had already moved to Atlanta.

Many people have asked me, "But shouldn't I only request benevolent outcomes for the important things?" What they're really asking is, "Am I bothering my guardian angel by making such a simple request?" I've learned over the past three years that these "whole souls" we call guardian angels have achieved a golden lightbeing level of knowledge and abilities. They are capable of making millions of decisions and giving a million pieces of advice each minute, and they don't take care of just one person but thousands of people every minute of the day and night. *Webster's Dictionary* defines the word benevolent as: "A kindly disposition to promote happiness and prosperity through good works, or by generosity in and pleasure of doing good works." That's exactly what your guardian angel wishes to do for you. Angels are most happy to assist you with even the smallest requests—but you have to request the assistance. They are not allowed to assist you unless you make the request!

So here's how most benevolent outcomes work:

- You must request the assistance.
- It must be benevolent not only for you but also for every-one connected to the request.
- It must be for you specifically. (Benevolent prayers are what you say for other people. I will explain those later on in this book.)
- It must be said out loud or in writing.
- There is no limit on the number of times you can request benevolent outcomes!

Benevolent Outcomes in Action

Jacqui in Australia emailed to say that she was going to renew her lease on an apartment (or flat, as they call it down under) in Melbourne and was really afraid they were going to increase the rent, as rents had been going up recently. So she requested a most benevolent outcome that she end up paying the same rent as she had been before. They renewed her lease with no increase! She said that that's unheard of right now in Melbourne.

Linda, who was really frightened, emailed from the New York area several times because she was out of work. I suggested several MBO requests to make, such as:

> *Most Benevolent Outcome*
>
> *"I request a most benevolent outcome for the perfect job for me. Thank you."*

and before interviews,

> *"I request a most benevolent outcome for this job interview, and may it go better than I can hope for or expect. Thank you!"*

She emailed not long after to tell me she'd gotten the job she'd applied for, and it was in her field of expertise: medical technical writing.

Paula writes: "I just bought five copies of *The Gentle Way* book and am thrilled that now I have presents to give. They will be birthday gifts for the people I love the most. I know your book has influenced me and I know the angels talk to us—if we would only listen. I use the benevolent requests daily and am still amazed with the results. I requested a parking space a few days ago. The wind was cold and raw, and I didn't want to walk those extra steps, but I also didn't want to end up in a spot where I would be getting my car banged up by other people's car doors. The angels found me a perfect spot with room galore, and it was three cars down from the doorway—perfect! And that's just one of many, many results I've had."

BG writes: "It seems people mostly report on the profound results they've received from using MBOs. I've had a couple of rather humorous but practical and useful results that I want to share. Ever since I moved into this new house four years ago, I have had trouble with the low-flow commodes working properly; therefore, the plunger is always close at hand. It is something I really dislike doing, but it beats the alternative. One day, even the plunger was unsuccessful. So I said, 'Well then, I request a most benevolent outcome for this commode to properly flush.' Nothing happened, so I walked away to contemplate calling a plumber. It wasn't long at all when I heard a gurgling sound coming from the bathroom. I went in to investigate, and sure enough, the commode was empty and flushing properly. During my meditation that week, I was reminded that the commode incident was metaphoric for how I hold on to 'junk.' So now I say an MBO as part of my daily constitutional: 'I request that I easily release and flush away the junk in my life.'

"Another MBO result happened this week when I had to park under a tree that was a popular spot for birds. I was on a tight schedule and did an MBO for a convenient spot that would let me get in and out quickly. When I got out and saw all the droppings, I debated moving, yet this was the most convenient—actually, the only—parking spot in the lot. So I requested an MBO for the bird droppings to miss my car. When I entered the door to the building where I was going, I looked back and saw there were no birds in the trees. I said thank you and went on about my business. I came out and still no birds. As I pulled out of the lot, I saw the birds return. Profundity comes in all shapes, huh?"

Di in the UK writes: "Last week I had two people email me on the same day to say they'd received *The Gentle Way* book (on my recommendation) and that they were astounded at how MBOs were happening for them. Also, someone in my corporate life whom I had advised to buy the book called to say he had been meaning for some time to say thank you. The book has changed his life, and his wife's I think they had been suffering from the credit crunch or thought they had been lacking. He mentioned that his friend's wife had been buying multiple copies of the book at a time to give to friends, saying: 'Just give this a try. Try asking for an MBO, and see how it works.' I had to write to tell you how your book is changing people's lives. How absolutely beautiful! I couldn't be more delighted. You must feel so proud, Tom! Your book changed my life, and I haven't stopped telling people since."

—————≫-◦-≪—————

I've been requesting benevolent outcomes for thirteen years, so I know they work from personal experience. I've requested MBOs somewhere around 15,000 times. When I did my first active meditation, I was told by a shaman from the 1600s that I had been a shaman myself and had also requested benevolent outcomes back then. I kept delving into the subject and was recently told that requesting benevolent outcomes dates back thousands of years before our recorded history. It's a simple way to live your life in a nonviolent manner, as if you stepped onto a much easier path to follow through life.

ARE THERE ANGELS OUT THERE?

Gail writes: "I've had so many blessings since asking for benevolent outcomes. A lot of people are doing intentions, but I find them limiting because I tend to blame myself when they fail, as if I hadn't been positive or sure enough. I like benevolent outcomes because you don't have to totally believe that the benevolent outcome will happen, which takes a lot of the pressure off. Also, I was raised Catholic and love angels. My question is, do you really feel there are angels out there, or is this just another way to do intentions? How did you come upon angels and start believing in them?"

—————≫-◦-≪—————

If you've read my book or my many newsletters, you know I believe in angels from knowledge and experience. That's the only true way to know for yourself. When I ask questions during my active meditations and receive thought-packet answers, many times the answer will be completely different than what I believed I would receive. That's when I know I'm tapped in. And it all started with requesting benevolent outcomes, seeing that there really was a wonderful being assisting me. It seemed over time to open up my awareness to listen for those whispers in my ear, knowing that it was not just my mind giving me the information.

Is There an Easier Way?

This person has requested that I not use her name. **Anonymous writes**: "Thankfully, I first read your articles in the *Sedona Journal of Emergence!* a few months ago. I immediately started to do MBOs and can see that they are helping in many ways. Now I share your technique and website with nearly all of my clients (I'm a clairvoyant reader), and many of them report great results! What kind of MBO would you say for when there are tremendous challenges and shifts on all levels, and it seems tricky and overwhelming to manage/juggle them all—yet in order to survive, there's no choice but to do all of them? I know it seems broad but challenges sometimes appear on every single level—work, health, finance, home, relationships, family—and all to such an intense degree that all need attention, change and evolution."

<hr/>

As Gaia once told me in meditation: "I don't wave a magic wand and 'poof,' things happen." I think it's the same way with requesting benevolent outcomes. Remember that one of the rules for requesting MBOs is that it has to be something specific for you. After requesting thousands of MBOs over the past thirteen years, if there were any shortcuts—or magic-wand waving!—I think I would have found them. But when I go out driving or when I work on specific business sales, when I've had medical issues or when I've wanted success in my personal life, I request an MBO each time for each specific thing.

I think MBOs were designed that way for a specific purpose, which I just finally learned recently. When you start requesting MBOs, you:

- Increase your awareness.
- Feel a lightening of spirit.
- Lower the level of fear in your life.
- Lower the level of stress in your life.
- Handle problems and challenges.
- Have more success in life.
- Raise your vibrational level.
- Increase your spirituality.

It may not be noticeable at first, but keep at it, and you'll see a difference. People are always asking, "How can I raise my vibrational level?" Requesting benevolent outcomes is the easiest, most fun and most gratifying way I've found so far. Everyone can do it, with no special training, rituals or anything else. Benevolent outcomes are for all of us!

ON REQUESTING BENVOLENT OUTCOMES MORE THAN ONCE

John writes: "Tom, I have been wondering how often one should repeat a request for a benevolent outcome, be it to your guardian angel or other beings, guides and masters. I have often read that to ask again and again undermines your request and shows a lack of faith. In other words, ask once and know it is done. Your thoughts?"

Sandi writes: "Jim and I have both been saying MBOs from your book, every morning: 'I request a most benevolent outcome that my personal established identity in all of its forms be safe and secure from harm and corruption by others,' and 'I request a most benevolent outcome that my computer hard drive and all my programs remain safe and secure from harm and corruption by others.' We got our credit card bill today and on it were long-distance phone calls from Germany totaling almost $350. While Jim was on the phone with the credit card company, another call was charged to our account. I requested an MBO for a positive outcome for us while he was on the phone trying to straighten this mess out. The charges are being dropped and we are being issued a new card. We are just wondering why the MBOs we request every morning didn't work."

—————>>-0-<<—————

Several of these letters came in on similar topics. Benevolent outcomes are to be requested for something specific for you, and my standard answer has always been—as I was told—that you only have to make the request one time. But still the letters kept coming, so I knew it was time to get a more direct answer from higher guidance. I asked my own guardian angel, Theo: "Should people only request a benevolent outcome once, or can they request the same MBO numerous times?"

Yes, if they feel a need to, they can request a benevolent outcome more than once, although it is not needed. One request works just as well as numerous requests. We, meaning what you call guardian angels, understand that since you are veiled, you question everything, even the validity of requesting MBOs, even when you have been having great success in requesting them. The veil is very thick, but it is thinning, and requesting MBOs thins the veil and raisers the vibrational level. So if people feel more comfortable in requesting a benevolent outcome more than once, it is okay. It will in no way dilute the request.

———◦———

So, in answer, request the same MBO as many times as you wish if it makes you feel more comfortable. Your guardian angel will not mind if you do. But do trust in the process. It works perfectly.

The Phrase "Any and All Beings"

If you wish to request something benevolent for someone else, you say what's called a benevolent prayer, as a whole different set of angels handle those prayers. You use the word "ask" because benevolent prayers are more general than the specific MBO requests you make for yourself. Over one million of the whole souls we call angels handle all the prayers said in the world—imagine their amazing capacities! When you request something benevolent for someone else, I normally recommend you say, "I ask any and all beings to _____." This is easy for everyone to remember and immediately draws the attention of one of the souls handling these prayers.

As an example, if your friend has a problem, you can say,

Benevolent Prayer

"I ask that any and all beings assist my friend with (whatever problem he/she is having) and may it be the most benevolent outcome for him/her. Thank you!"

For another example, if there is some tragedy in the world—say, an earthquake—and you wish you could do something for the people who are affected, but you aren't able to, you could say,

Benevolent Prayer

"I ask that any and all beings assist the people in (city or country) who are trapped, so that they may be rescued. Thank you!"

You use the phrase "any and all beings" because this could mean a man, woman, child, rescue dog, cat or even an angel become physical—anyone who might assist in manifesting a benevolent outcome. I guarantee you'll feel better just by saying this simple prayer.

In this book you'll read many more stories, some that have happened in my life, and many more that have happened in other people's lives, all from people who have adopted these simple methods of making life less stressful, less fearful and more successful. And as I requested in my first book, say this out loud now:

Most Benevolent Outcome

"I request a most benevolent outcome for reading this book, and may the results be even better than I can hope for or expect. Thank you!"

Try requesting benevolent outcomes. Just as the many people in this book have discovered, I think you too will find a benevolent universe waiting for you.

CHAPTER ONE

BENEVOLENT OUTCOMES
AROUND TOWN

My daughter was married on a Saturday in June, and anyone who's gone through this experience knows how stressful it can be. So here are some benevolent outcomes that happened through our requests.

First was my wife's search for a dress for the ceremony. As Dena and I work together in our business, this meant we both had to take off from work to look for one. Both she and I requested a benevolent outcome for quickly finding the perfect dress for her and that it would be better than we hoped or expected. In Dallas there's a store named Terry Costa that sells all sorts of beautiful gowns and dresses for all occasions. The owner is the ex-wife of Victor Costa, the designer. After arriving, we went directly to the sale section, as we didn't feel the dress would be worn again for some time, if ever. We found a beautiful dress that was originally offered at around $300 and was on sale for $120. Then the sales woman, to our surprise, took off another 50 percent to drop it to $60! It still needed altering, but so would any of the other dresses.

Next, my son and I went to pick up our tuxes on Thursday. Naturally, I requested an MBO for the drive there, and that the tuxes would fit properly. They did fit well, and we left to return a bad laser printer to Fry's Electronics store, which was about an eight-minute drive north. As we were walking into the store, my daughter called and said the store had called her to say that I had left my tuxedo shirt on the chair there. I was surprised, but sent my son in to get the printer while I drove back to the store, wondering why I hadn't received a benevolent outcome. When I arrived, the owner said that our handkerchiefs had just arrived. I'm quite sure he forgot to give them to us, so it was a good MBO that I had to return while I was still nearby. When I arrived back at Fry's, they still hadn't found the printer, which was the only one left on sale. Both my son and I requested MBOs, and finally, after another thirty minutes, they found the printer we wanted behind several other boxes of printers. Also, when my wife went out searching for a rehearsal dinner dress (after requesting a benevolent outcome), she immediately found one on sale for $22—and it looked great!

A Wedding Reception

Cheri writes: "I really enjoy your newsletter and pass it on to friends. I have been using MBOs sort of on and off since I saw you in Texas a couple of months ago. I wanted to tell you that my roommate (a dear friend) and I recently had a very powerful demonstration of the effectiveness of MBOs. Her daughter and her husband, originally married in a civil ceremony three years ago, were planning to celebrate their union with a marriage blessing in their church. Our extended family was very excited about the upcoming celebration and had been preparing for some time. There was just one problem.

Due to a very limited budget and the high cost of renting a space, there were no plans for a reception after the ceremony. The plans, though lovely, felt truncated, and we all longed for a way to bring this special occasion to a more appropriate conclusion. After exploring all conceivable options, we had finally, reluctantly, given up.

"One week to the day before the ceremony, my roommate had a thought (divinely inspired) about a room at her church that might be available for free. Four days and many prayers later, she confirmed that we had the room. That left all of us just three days to put the reception together after work. For every obstacle we met, there were answers. Resources, ideas and people appeared just when we needed them. It took a lot of work and some close episodes, but the next Saturday night after a beautiful ceremony, we had a great reception. Almost everyone who attended the wedding was able to be there, even beloved friends who were attending another function at the same church and were drawn to our event. Thus, the happy couple got to celebrate their commitment to each other in the company of family and friends."

—◦—

I would have advised Cheri to request a benevolent outcome when they had the problem, and very probably the solution to the problem would have presented itself earlier, or perhaps an even better solution. They co-created the solution through synchronicity. You'll find this happening more and more as we move into the fifth dimension.

Shorten a Waiting Line

Laurie writes: "I'm going to relate an MBO success story. I ask for pretty mundane things, and this one is no different, but the result was pretty significant, relatively speaking. I dislike going to my main post office branch because the line is usually so long and slow. But this time I was forced to go there because I wanted to rent a PO Box. I asked for an MBO for a short line about a half hour before going to the post office, and lo and behold, there were only about six or seven people in line when I got there. Unheard of! That fact was reinforced to me when the next person in line behind me remarked that she'd never seen the line so short. The universe was telling me, 'See!'"

———✦———

The way this request probably worked was Laurie's guardian angel contacted other guardian angels whose "clients" would have been in line at that time so that they would either come a few minutes early, or delay their trip to the post office for a few minutes. Isn't it neat the way that works?

On the Freeway

Linda writes: "Yesterday, before leaving to go to a friend's house, I requested an MBO for a safe return home. While driving down the I-75 local freeway, I realized I was going 55 miles per hour. I thought to myself, 'That's ridiculous,' and decided to speed up. At that moment, as we went into a curve, a black SUV with Georgia plates came into my lane and completed the whole curve, halfway in my lane. Had I been driving at my normal speed, she would have taken me out. As I regained my composure, I dutifully thanked my guardian angel. I watched this person take an exit off the freeway, and I sent love to her in her oblivion of what had almost changed our lives. Funny how we affect others without even realizing. Thank you."

And that's also an example of the radiant effect in which your MBO request affects others: the other driver was kept safe too.

At the Laundromat

Jan writes: "After my ordeal last week at the Laundromat, when the two ladies running the place refused to turn on the air conditioner, I refused to go back. This week I mentioned needing to wash laundry, but I refused to go back to that place. My daughter pointed out that a new Laundromat had recently opened, one that was closer to me, and that I should check on that one first.

"I immediately said 'I request the most benevolent outcome that the new laundromat is open and that I have a good experience there. Thank you, angels.' I got the clothes ready and messed around for a little while, then headed to the new Laundromat. From the parking lot I could see a lady inside doing her laundry. So I got out and went in. Yes, they were open. They had been open about thirty minutes when I got there. The owner told me the inspectors had just left and said they could open for business. Amazing!"

LOST AND FOUND

A few days ago I took my dogs for their afternoon walk. Normally my wife walks them too, but she was super busy, so I went alone. As I rounded the bend a half-block from my house, I looked down and spied a red object on the sidewalk, something partially hidden by monkey grass. I reached down to find a red cell phone that someone had dropped. I didn't have my reading glasses on, so I couldn't see the numbers. I wondered how I'd get in touch with the person who had dropped it, and thought perhaps one of my children would find a way. But just to be safe, I requested a benevolent outcome out loud to find the person the cell phone belonged to. I continued on my walk. A few minutes later, the cell phone rang and I answered. It was the owner's husband. I told him I had it and gave instructions for how to find my house. About forty-five minutes later, he showed up and explained that his wife dropped it while walking their dog. They live only two blocks from us. If she had been searching, it would have been very difficult to see the cell phone in the shadows of the trees and grass.

Kelly writes: "I was returning from grocery shopping and while driving noticed that my cell phone was missing. It wasn't where I usually put it (in the outer pocket of my purse), nor was it in my coat pocket—the second most likely spot. I was already a bit stressed from a full workday followed by shopping and knowing I had hungry mouths at home to feed, and I dreaded the thought of having to retrace my steps.

"Well, I immediately requested an MBO for my cell phone to be in the car. As soon as I pulled into the garage, I heard a phone ringing; I immediately thought the angels were letting me know I could relax as the phone was in the car; it was just a matter of locating it. Sure enough, it was in the trunk. How it got there, I can't imagine—besides, I rarely get calls on it. Weeks pass without a single call. It is only for emergencies. I thought then that maybe my husband had called. No. The caller ID showed an unknown number and an area code I wasn't familiar with. No message, just a missed call. The timing was impeccable. The ring happened literally within two minutes of my request. Divine intervention? I sure think so!"

Kelly adds: "It seems that I actually experienced a sort of layering effect with my MBOs last evening. Prior to my grocery shopping, I requested an MBO that I'd be able to accomplish all I had planned at the store: finding what I had intended, finding a perfect parking spot, lots of space in the store and a quick-moving checkout line and no crowds so that I could get home swiftly and be able to put dinner together in a relaxed manner without time pressure.

"Well, the phone ringing in the car immediately let me know I didn't have to go back to the store (more time for me!). You see, it was in the trunk, but not visible. It was quite dark and under a bag. I wouldn't have seen it, nor would I have looked in the trunk, of all places, had it not rung. I can just imagine if it hadn't rung—I would have gone back to the store looking, a fruitless search, not knowing it was in the trunk.

"I believe the angels were working on the MBO I'd previously requested, that I have a leisurely dinner prep time. In fact, it gets better. My fourteen-year-old son approached me at the door and was very upbeat, saying 'I love you, Mom,' repeatedly—more than usual. It seemed to instill a leisurely and calming mood in me after such a busy day. In fact, he willingly helped me make dinner, an all-new occurrence. So all of these situations show how this request for a leisurely time was honored too. I am so grateful! Thank you so much for introducing this concept to the world. It is wonderful. Many, many thanks."

Helena in London writes: "I left my flat to go to work but decided to go back to get my diary; in my rush and absent-mindedness after locking up my flat, I went out the communal door and put my rucksack on top of the dustbin shelter. Unbeknownst to me, I also put my flat keys down while I opened my bag to put the diary in. Off I dashed to work (bear in mind I had done my MBOs that morning). One of my morning MBOs involves asking that my home remain safe from intrusion, an MBO you recommended in your first book, Tom.

"My day went by, and I worked late that Friday evening, so when I locked the surgery up, I could not find my house keys. I searched everywhere. One of the receptionists was kind enough to help me search, but we could not find them anywhere. This made me panic; I couldn't concentrate and started to fear the worst, so Heather, the other receptionist, offered to come home with me.

"I started to feel quite negative in my thinking: "My flat's been broken into," or "The neighbors have got my keys and have gone up into my flat." Under the circumstances I would have just burst into tears, but for some reason I didn't. On the way home I started pleading to the angels for help and I started requesting MBOs. I didn't care what my friend thought, though she was giggling and teasing me for the things I was requesting —and she looked at me in a strange way, but I did not care! She probably thought I had lost my marbles.

"I couldn't believe it, but as I got nearer to my flat I saw my keys, just sitting there on top of the dustbin shelter! I could not believe they were still there, as a whole day had passed, and it's a busy street—anyone could have taken them. My God, my requesting of MBOs definitely worked for me. I thanked everyone and every thing for my keys and my flat being safe! Wow, Tom, aren't I sure one lucky person? Thank you!"

———•—•—•———

Helena had her guardian angel acting as a security guard for her all day!

LOST AND FOUND, CONTINUED

Laurie writes: "My mom came home from the grocery store and realized she didn't have her purse. It's a small clutch, not a big handbag. After some confusion and worry, she remembered what I'd told her about MBOs and asked God and the angels to help her find her purse. She didn't use the exact language of "I request a most benevolent outcome for . . ." but the message went out. She returned to the grocery store parking lot two hours later (having first cancelled all her credit cards just in case), and while she and one of the managers were combing the area where she'd parked, the fellow bringing in the shopping carts came up to them. He held up my mom's little clutch purse and said: "Are you looking for this?" Not only had he found the clutch, he'd found it only a few minutes before encountering my mom. It had been wedged in the flip-up seat of the grocery cart—nicely hidden. Thank you, guardian angels! What a great case of synchronicity. The purse had been sitting in the cart out in the parking lot for two hours before my mom, the manager and the cart-collecting employee all merged. Wow! I write fiction for a living, but if I wrote this incident in a story, an editor would say it was contrived."

Planning and Making Appointments

Harry is a masseuse. He forgot to write an appointment down, so he overbooked and had to change his appointment at a credit union at the last minute. I've condensed his story for space.

Harry writes: "I asked if I could come in [to the credit union] in the morning, before noon—at 10:00 AM. She said that they had a staff meeting at nine, and if I could be there by ten, it would be fine. I went into overdrive—had to flush my pool filter before I left, take a shower and pack my massage chair, oils, towels and so on into my car. I got in the car at 9:20 AM, and as soon as I put the key in and turned on the car, my gas gauge beeped at me. I realized that I had forgotten to fill up the night before. I quickly asked for an MBO of the events taking place and headed to the gas station around the corner. At the gas station I scanned my discount card and my debit card and waited. The screen popped up with a "Problem—See Attendant" message. I went and called the attendant and he said that the computer was running slowly that morning and that I should re-enter everything. It worked the second time, and after filling my car, I hit the road. My clock read 9:29 AM, and I was running late.

"Out loud I said, 'Okay guys. I really need a most benevolent outcome with a little time warp to get me to my destination as quickly and safely as possible without breaking any laws. Please keep all traffic lights green so I can get there expeditiously!' As I passed each green traffic light, I shouted thank you—this happened thirteen times! Then, as I approached the next light, it turned red. As I slowed to a stop, I said aloud, 'Thank you for letting me catch a breather and drink some water.' I continued on through Garland into East Dallas and made every other traffic light—I quit counting; I just kept shouting thank you. I entered the credit union parking lot at 9:58 to another rousing thank you!"

SHOPPING

Lynn writes: "I said an MBO yesterday for an area where I feel blocked. Last night I had a dream where I felt this get unblocked, as I experienced a situation and felt things being released in the dream. So now I realize if I request an MBO, it can work on any level—in the physical, but also in dream worlds.

"Today I rang the people who deliver a fruit and veggie box to us each fortnight and remembered just as I was being put through to quickly say an MBO. I told the customer service person that our fruit from them had been bad, and that I wasn't satisfied. She gave me 50 percent off our next box! I also found out how to know what's in our box in advance—a real help for us.

"Also, on a weekend outing to do a small job at a shopping center, I asked for an MBO and afterward I saw how many good outcomes there were—if I said them all here, it would take up a page. The job I did went really well. The person I was working with had a very good rapport with me—we had a very good exchange, which is unusual for people doing her particular job. A man came up to us in our car as we were leaving, asking for some money to buy petrol, so Michael gave him a few dollars, and I later saw him at a gas station with the hood up and a petrol can in his hand, so his request was genuine. So MBOs even work for helping others."

Dining Room Set Sale

Jackie in Plano, Texas writes: "I had a dining room set for sale for over a month. I advertised on craigslist and at work on our internal newsletter. It missed the July publication, and I was upset because I needed the money. Then a close friend, John L., forwarded your newsletter and I thought I would try it. I only said one MBO. My ad came in the August newsletter at work and in less than fifteen minutes, I got an email from a coworker in the IT department, and he came over that evening to buy it. I was able to pay four bills that were due with the money I made, and I even bought a new purse, since I had noticed the night before that the old one was beginning to tear at the zipper! Now I say the phrase about expecting great things every day. It really works when you get out of the way and have faith that your angels really will do the best for you. Thank you, thank you, thank you, Tom."

Marble Tile Deal

Anne Marie writes on Facebook: "Tom, I have to tell you about my friend's MBO. She is redoing her bathroom and wanted real marble tiles. Well, a 12 x 12 inch square normally goes for anywhere from $10 to $15.

So on Sunday, after doing an MBO in church, she drove to Lowe's. As she was walking to the tile aisle, on the end of the aisle were boxes of tiles with a sign: 'Marble—only $1.42 each tile.' She was speechless and felt it must be a mistake. Then the salesman showed up and told her they were overstocked in those tiles. They were not selling and his boss said 'mark 'em down.' At that price she told him she could do both bathrooms and had measurements requiring twenty boxes. He told her that if she bought them right then, he would discount the price to $1.00 per square—now that is an MBO! Most benevolent outcomes for the best possible deal, yeah!"

CELEBRITY SIGHTINGS

Dianne writes: "The three ladies in my office and I passed an insurance examination this year. I can tell you I needed all the MBOs you could possibly imagine during the studying and the actual exam—thank the angels we all passed. In recognition of all our hard work, and our eventual success, we were rewarded by our company to a meal at a top London restaurant. We were booked to attend the Wolseley Restaurant (which was built in the 1930s, I believe, as the showroom for the new Wolseley motor car). In honor of this prestigious car, the showrooms were designed in the Venetian/Florentine architecture of the Art Deco period, featuring marble, sweeping staircases and ornate mirrors. The Wolseley is situated opposite the Ritz in the heart of the Piccadilly/Mayfair area of London and apparently it is the haunt of many well-known celebrities.

"I did not know that this was the reason the restaurant had been chosen for us. However, my manager, who accompanied us, was desperate to see and, most of all, meet a celebrity. He complained all evening that we were dining too early and that we wouldn't be able to see a celebrity from where our table was if any did happen to arrive. I, on the other hand, was having a wonderful evening, having previously asked for an MBO. The venue and food were first-class and the atmosphere quite warm and friendly—quite often these places can feel intimidating. Anyway, no celebrities.

"Finally we were ready to leave, and my manager Paul—who was desperate to see a celebrity much more than any of us four ladies—another woman and I went to the restrooms. We went down one of the sweeping staircases to the lower floor where they were located, one at a time. I was the last down the stairs when all of a sudden I heard a woman shout. I knew it wasn't my friend, but I was concerned that she was okay, so I rushed to the door I'd seen her disappear through. In the doorway with her back to me was a woman laughing and talking to Jane (my friend) who stood behind her. The lady had thought Jane was someone she knew and had shouted in surprise at seeing her there (incidentally, no one was more surprised than Jane). When the woman turned around and I could see her face, she was none other than a famous UK celebrity and television presenter. She apologized for delaying me in the doorway and then left. Jane and I held on to one another laughing so hard, because here was our celebrity and we had practically bumped into her.

"Well, it didn't stop there. Oh no. The angels had more surprises in store. I went into the cubicle only to find a mobile phone, a pair of sunglasses and a cardigan on the shelf. When we went back upstairs, I found our server and gave her all the stuff, telling her about the woman who had just left the restroom before us and asking if these could possibly be hers. They were and she was very grateful for them to be returned—especially her phone, as you can imagine. I had such a wonderful evening, Tom, and would have enjoyed myself without meeting my new celebrity friend; however, she was the icing on the cake, and such a fantastic MBO—one that I would never have imagined myself. It was just so funny when we told Paul what had happened. You couldn't believe the look on his face. I can still see it now. So I said, 'I told you but you didn't believe me, did you? If you want to meet a celebrity, you request an MBO.' I'm still laughing from the whole thing. How funny, eh?"

Parking and Fireworks

Pamela in California writes: "I have some MBOs for you. I used the parking one and asked for, 'something better than I could wildly imagine.' The first time, a couple was pulling out of a space and the meter still had one hour of time left on it. The second time, as I was figuring out whether or not I had enough money for the meter, I noticed that it was out of order. Another one was last Saturday: A male friend invited me over to his place for a home-cooked meal. Again, I asked for 'something better than I could imagine' following my MBO request. Well, we were sitting on his beautiful balcony, looking right out over the water and boats in Marina del Rey, when suddenly this beautiful fireworks show began right in front of us. Fireworks are one of my most favorite things. My friend exclaimed that he had never seen them from that direction and had no idea where they were coming from. We both jokingly decided it was because it was 'Pam Day,' and we made it a holiday."

Discounts and Ease in Shopping

Lynn from Oregon writes: "I wanted to share this part of a letter my friend Annie sent me. She had made a trip to Phoenix to take care of her ninety-year-old father who needed some dental work. She lives up in a small mountain town, but used to live in Phoenix. So when she comes into town, she tries to get a lot of things done, things that a small town does not offer.

I introduced her to MBOs by sending her a copy of your book. As you can see, she has become a great believer."

From Annie in Arizona: "The rest of my trip after taking care of Dad was pretty good and full of MBOs. I needed to shop, since there is no place in our little town that sells some of the items I needed. I did get three bras on sale at Kohl's on senior's day, with the senior discount to boot, and a smoking deal on blue jeans too. I needed bras and was going to buy them no matter what the price. The first Kohl's only had one in my size, and it was on the bottom rack, way in the back—you know how it is when you have to have one specific brand/style. I even had to squat down to find it. Off I went to another Kohl's, asking for an MBO for at least two of them. I walked into the department and there were two of them on the front of the rack, chest high. I continued to ask for MBOs for all my errands and got prime parking spaces and all my stuff in no time at all. The oral surgeon was even early, the wait for Dad's return transport was faster than usual and I had a safe, quick trip home. What a deal! I thanked the universe and angels profusely."

I guess that was a "BBO"—a bra benevolent outcome!

Personal Beauty and Time Compression

Kelly writes: "Yesterday I requested an MBO for going to visit my hairstylist. She was a new stylist for me; the other two times I'd visited her there was a stiffness between us, not much talking going on. It felt uncomfortable and not nearly as relaxed as with my prior stylist of thirteen years, but this new woman did good work. I requested that my visit go smoothly and comfortably between us and that a mutual rapport would begin so that my future visits with her would be comfortable and something to look forward to.

"As I sat down at the shampoo sink, our conversation hit off with a bang from a mere comment I made about feeling chilled despite the spring weather. It just so happens she and I both have that tendency, and then that led to other topics that revealed other common traits between us. In fact, the haircut went by in a breeze, and I was so into the discussion that I didn't realize she was done. We both were laughing and smiling. What a great outcome!

"I also want to share some incidents involving compression of time I have experienced. I can't recall the exact wording I used; I believe I said something like, 'I request that time stretch out to allow me to get to my class on time, without feeling stressed or panicked, and with sufficient time to allow for preparing my kids' dinner before leaving.' It worked marvelously. I was on my way home from work during rush hour and had forty-five minutes until class time—the trip home could take twenty to thirty minutes at times—or as little as fifteen. Then the class was five minutes from my house, but I had to change and prepare dinner. I had seven minutes to spare once I got to class! (I didn't look at the clock during my trip, either).

"Another incident involved a trip into Chicago for a class. I rarely drive downtown and felt I left sufficient time, but didn't realize that road construction nearby was really slowing traffic. I put the request to use again—again, though, I forget the exact wording. Apparently it worked; I had fifteen minutes to spare and made sure I left earlier the next day of the class so I wouldn't cut it so close. The next time I was on my way home from my course, I hit rush hour. I had previously requested a rapid trip home to allow for extra non-rushed time that evening to unwind before thinking about the next day's work. As I approached the ramp to the express lanes (as I said, I rarely drive downtown and tend to avoid the express lanes), I had to decide if I'd take the ramp or stay on the regular route. It just so happens I was listening to a Deepak Chopra CD, and at precisely the last moment I could make the decision, Deepak, in his discussion of time/timelessness, mid-sentence said, 'Take the fast lane.' I abruptly did and the pace of traffic was smooth and flowing much faster than the regular route. It did slow up a bit later, but I did make it home earlier than I had thought and was able to unwind with my kids and chat with a friend. Now I will keep a memo for myself in the car to request a compression of time—fewer words and a lot easier to say."

<hr />

Notice how her guardian angel arranged for the CD to play that particular part at just the right time. Those are the moments when you know that your guardian angel is chuckling! And don't forget to say, "I request a compression of time, thank you!" whenever you need more time.

Your Bank Account

Annette writes: "I was not going to tell you about the first part of this story, but since the second part is too weird and has to be part of the MBO I've requested for assistance in paying down my debts, here goes. I forgot to get buns for the bratwurst we were having for dinner and had to run to the grocery up the

road. While there, I overheard the cashiers talking about putting ice in a cart of food and looking for a missing card. When I
went outside, there was a woman and her daughter sitting in the
chairs on display out front. The woman was on the cell phone
crying hysterically—as I walked toward my car, I heard a voice
tell me to turn around. I did and walked over to the woman.

She was off the phone and crying even harder. I asked if
there was something I could do, and the woman took my hand
and thanked me for my concern but that there was nothing
I could do. Then she started crying too hard to speak. Her
daughter, who must have been in her late teens, told me they'd
lost their grocery gift-card and hadn't realized it was missing
until they were checking out. They'd called home and no one
could find it; they didn't have any money for the groceries. I
asked them how much their groceries were and the daughter
said 'Probably a hundred dollars.' I thought for a moment and
decided I could help them with fifty dollars. The mother, still
holding my hand, looked at me in shock as I said 'Come on.
Let's get the groceries.' I got the head cashier, and they pulled
out some things that were 'extra,' and the cashier had someone
take the cold food back. As they rang it up, the mother kept
hugging me and thanking me and telling me I would be paid
back and that I was an angel.

"They had potatoes, chicken, vegetables, cooking oil, a few
buy-one-get-one-free sodas, ice cream and a pack of breakfast
rolls. As they got to the end of their groceries, the mother told
the daughter to put back the ice cream and the breakfast rolls
and I told her, 'No, go ahead and get those.' I was not going to
deny them a little comfort food. The amount came to around
sixty dollars, but I knew I could swing it if I just took my lunch
a few more times over the following two weeks and didn't buy

anything unnecessary. As we were leaving, a young pregnant girl met them. I was introduced to their preacher's wife who, the woman told me, was going to join them for dinner. We exchanged numbers and hugs and I went on home. When I told my husband, he was amazingly cool with it and actually felt we'd be fine. I did too.

"Now here is where it gets weird. I had balanced our checking and savings accounts the day before, to the penny. This morning (Tuesday), I opened the account to transfer money from savings to checking for my husband and there was sixty dollars more in there than was there on Saturday. I checked the account, and there had been no deposit, no explanation, nothing. Now, I could have made a mistake and not noticed I had sixty dollars in savings, but . . . Now isn't that a most benevolent outcome?"

<hr />

Yes, it's nice to know that a guardian angel can put money into your account!

A GUARDIAN ANGEL TAKES THE WHEEL

Daphnee writes: "I happened to read the part of your newsletter regarding the guardian angels embodying in 3D to save someone's life. A few years ago while living in Cyprus, I was driving very fast in the fast lane and overtook two cars in the middle lane. There was a third car ahead in the slow lane— I was about to overtake this car and was slightly ahead of it already, when suddenly, invisible hands grabbed the wheel and I found myself slowing down and dropping behind the car I actually had already overtaken.

"In the same moment, a car came from the opposite direction toward me in the lane I was before. I don't know how you call this in English, but in German we call that a 'ghost rider.' I don't know what happened, but I knew it was not me. 'Daphnee' would never have slowed down and moved over to the slow lane, especially as I had already passed the other car. I thought, 'Oh, was that my guardian angel?'

"This is the event in my life where I started to believe in angels and dared talking to mine. For years I have not been sure: do I have one only or many? My feeling is that it's a plural form of angel, but I am not sure. Maybe you can shed some light on that?"

———⊳·◦·⊲———

There is only one golden lightbeing whom we call our guardian angel who oversees us every minute of the day and night. We do have one or two main guides, as well as several, that come and go depending upon what we're doing at that time in life.

By an Eyelash

Judy in Sydney, Australia, writes: "I just have to tell you about my recent angel miracle. On Tuesday night, I was going to a night class in another part of Sydney. I said my MBOs for safe travel before I left. When I got there, I parked my car and walked across the street with the green light. Suddenly, an elderly lady in a 4WD flew around the corner at full speed and narrowly missed me—I mean, by an eyelash! She said she was looking at the lights and not at pedestrians on the crosswalk. I screamed and fell back into the road, but I only scraped my hand and got a few bruises.

"Several people ran to give me their cards as witnesses but I really was all right, just shaken up. Another quarter of a second and I would have been badly hit. After my class, I stopped off at the supermarket and playing over the loudspeaker was the song, 'Send Me an Angel.' How's that for confirmation? I can't thank you enough for your instructions with MBOs—it saved my life!"

WHO DO YOU ADDRESS?

Sandy writes: "Hello Tom, thank you so much for your information on benevolent outcomes. I think I've been using it for many years, only never using the specific words 'request' and 'benevolent.' Anyway, I would like to ask a question: When beginning the request, who do you address? I seem to get in the way of myself, using angels, universe, God, All That Is, higher self, energy and so on. It seems, from what I can tell from your articles, that there is no direction for addressing one entity and that our request just starts out as, 'I request a most benevolent outcome for . . .' Is this correct? Does All That Is know who we're speaking to? Then, when I say thanks, it seems I want to thank the universe. Will you please comment on this? Thanks so much for your uplifting advice. I've shared this with family; it is so positive and loving to use."

<hr/>

I've been told that addressing angels, Creator, God, archangels and so on just gets in the way and can even limit your request. When you request an MBO, keep in mind that your guardian angel is monitoring you every minute of the day, as it has great capabilities far beyond even my understanding (and I've been asking questions for four years now), so when you say, "I request . . . ," that immediately tells your guardian angel that you're requesting an MBO. Even though it knows your thoughts in advance, you have to say it out loud and with emotion, if possible.

You don't have to, but I always thank my guardian angel at the end of the request. That's just showing your love and respect for what this beautiful being volunteered for, millions of years ago, Earth time: to be of service to us, as we have these hard, challenging lives, completely veiled from knowing who we really are. And when the MBO is granted, I thank my guardian angel three times; again, this is my way of acknowledging and recognizing the assistance I received.

A FEW REMINDERS ABOUT YOUR ANGEL

Your guardian angel is always trying to let you know it's there to assist you. Most of the time you ignore these reminders. Even though I communicate with Theo in my active meditations, he still likes to surprise me with reminders, which I think he does so that I'll relate them to you! One of the ways he does this is by having certain songs played on the radio, or he'll have me remember a specific song when I awake in the morning. Last Sunday my wife and I were over at our new house, which is still undergoing remodeling. Finally, after my wife was satisfied she had made sufficient notes to relay to the contractor, we closed up the building and got in our car for the return trip to our old house. Just as I turned on the car engine, the car radio started playing one of my favorite songs—"Fooled Around and Fell in Love" by the Elvin Bishop band with vocals by Mickey Thompson, who earned a spot in the band Jefferson Starship based on this performance. It was "by request" and I told my wife at the time that yes, it was Theo's request. So in my next meditation I asked Theo a few questions.

Theo, I assume that was you that arranged for the Elvin Bishop song to be played as I turned on the car engine this past Sunday?

Yes, of course it was. I simply arranged, as you guessed, with another guardian angel who takes care of a client who likes the same song to have him call the radio station and request it. That was a simple job or action for us to do.

Well, I thank you, Theo. It was enjoyable for both my wife and I to sing along, and thank the other guardian angel for its assistance too.

I will, Tom. That's nice of you to think about too.

❋   ❋   ❋

So pay attention to those reminders, folks! Your own guardian angel is saying, "Don't forget about me—I'm here to assist you; you just have to ask!"

DON'T FORGET TO MAKE THE REQUEST

Requesting benevolent outcomes has to become a habit or you'll forget to request MBOs when you most need them. The more you request, the more fun life will be, as reader Ellen discovers.

Ellen writes: "On Mother's Day here in Canada our church provided the gift of bedding plants donated by a local nursery. They looked pretty worn, but I picked a four-pack of pansies. I asked for a benevolent outcome when I planted them in poor weather. They are doing beautifully and are fresh and healthy.

"That was the second time I asked for an MBO. The first time was amazing. Medical insurance here is free, but waiting for an appointment except in an emergency is long. I had been trying since April to get an appointment for a checkup in May and then in June, which didn't work out. Finally, on Friday three weeks ago, I had just read your article and asked for the doctor's office to call saying they had found an appointment for me in June. Ninety minutes later, the receptionist called to tell me my appointment would be on June 11. That made a believer out of me."

I responded to Ellen: Be sure to request benevolent outcomes for everything in your daily life, so you won't forget to request an MBO when you really need one. This is a habit that must be formed, or you'll eventually forget and go back to just being the ping-pong ball bouncing back and forth from hit after hit.

CHAPTER TWO

BENEVOLENT OUTCOMES AT HOME

Diane writes: "I just had to share what happened the other day. It had me smiling myself to sleep and feeling so great and grateful. The other day when we got home, my husband told me that he could not find his wedding ring. He has a habit in the morning of taking his watch and ring off before he takes his shower. When he finished his shower, his watch was there, but no ring. He looked everywhere, including on the floor and under the bed, but there was no sign of the ring. So he went to work without his ring. It bothered him, of course, and when I got home. I looked for the ring too but turned up nothing. The ring was nowhere to be seen. So I immediately said my most benevolent outcome request.

"Well, we got into bed and were getting ready to go to sleep. My husband had the TV on and was lying on his side when all of the sudden, he felt something cold on his leg. He put his hand near his leg, and what did he find? His ring! He was surprised and all he could say was: 'I can't believe it.' All I could say was thank you while smiling from ear to ear for the answer to my prayer: 'I request a most benevolent outcome for finding David's ring. Thank you.'

"I also added one thing that my mom taught me always works: 'Nothing is lost in Spirit.' I said both of them and then just relaxed. I had to share this with you because I felt good, happy, excited and very grateful. I have thanked my angels a million times. After this miracle I also realized you shouldn't worry and fret when you can just trust in God and your angels and all will be well. Your angels want to help you, and they can't unless you call.

"I'm still working on the most benevolent outcome for selling my home, improving my credit and getting some extra money so that we can move with no problem. I have a strong feeling that I will get what I want in the selling of my home, even in this down market. I refuse to go with the market or believe negative talk about not getting the price I want. So far, some folks I have contacted have given me low amounts, but I refuse to be discouraged. I'm holding strong in faith, knowing that I will get the amount I want and need for the house. My angels will come through for me, I just know it! Thank you so much. I'm now on the start of great things."

For those of you who have read my first book, you know that I had a similar experience. I realized after we'd left a movie theater that I didn't have my wedding ring on. When we arrived back home, I called the theater and they searched to no avail. I was quite concerned because I had lost my first wedding ring during a Boy Scout canoe trip, and I didn't want to lose my second one. I looked all over the house and couldn't find it, even requesting a benevolent outcome. Then my wife went to her bathroom and found my ring where it had slipped off while quickly washing my hands before running out the door for the movie. Also, my wife and I have both requested benevolent outcomes for selling our house at a good price too, so we're patiently waiting without fear.

Home Repair and Getting a New Car

Jacquie writes: "A great many changes have occurred following my request for MBOs. During a night of heavy wind and a downpour of rain, my living room ceiling began to leak. Retired and getting by, I asked for an MBO. After all was said and done, I needed something in the neighborhood of $25,000 of work done on my cottage. Other needed work came to light when they came to inspect the roof, so it was all taken care of at one time. I'll be at town hall tomorrow to wrap up paperwork on the completion of this work. It would take another paragraph to list everything that was done. The work was funded through a Federal program called the Small Towns Program, for those aged sixty-five and older.

"As if that was not enough, I needed a new car. Affording this is not a walk in the park with my retirement salary and identity theft issues. I am now driving the 2008 Honda Civic of my dreams. Oh, I forgot, I also received almost $3,000 out of the blue too. You couldn't make this up. Who would believe you? I am grateful to a benevolent universe, to myself for allowing miracles and to my super-duper guardian angel and angelic guides.

"The above was written some weeks ago. I've been unable to send it to your email until now, and I hope this one goes through. By way of overkill, I will add that since the above was written I have received the notice of my stimulus check (as have many), and another notice from the department I retired from that I will be receiving $2,000 from a union settlement. There's a lot I want to do. I keep reassuring myself that this is okay and that magic and miracles are our true nature."

Avoiding Termites

Vicki in Texas writes: "I did want to let you know about another MBO related to termites. We had a termite swarm appear in our Jacuzzi tub. The pest guy with twenty years of experience chasing bugs came to check them out. He was very knowledgeable and had all these ideas about where the bugs would be coming from. Both my husband and myself said MBOs for the termite problem. When the bug guy returned to treat the termites, he could find no trace of a current termite problem. He seems like the kind of technician who always finds the bugs, so when he could not find any bugs, he was totally baffled. I know it was due to the MBOs. I am hopeful that my husband's cancer will go the way of the termites. Thanks again for your newsletters, advice and most of all for introducing us to MBOs."

Norine writes: "I've had several interesting MBOs happen since I've started making requests. But here's another 'is this really possible?' story for you. I have an air filter/purifier in my bedroom that I use nightly. It's old, but I keep it because it has a particular hum to it that I've gotten used to, and it helps me sleep. The model isn't one they even make anymore, because people like the quieter ones, but you can still get replacement filters for the old model.

"The other night, I turned on the air filter and I heard a weird noise, like a motor dying, and after that it didn't work. I tried turning it on and off several times to no avail. That night I found falling asleep to be a little difficult because I didn't have the soothing hum of the machine. So I asked for an MBO that by tomorrow night it might be working again (I mean, I had just spent $100 on the replacement filters a couple months before and hated to have them go to waste.)

"Tom, the next night when I turned the air filter on, it was working—unbelievable! Thank you, thank you, thank you! Who knows, maybe it will just keep working until I use all the purchased filters up. I not only have a mechanical guardian angel, but she's ecological, too!"

A REQUEST FOR SLEEP

Julie writes: "Tom, I have had trouble falling asleep most of my life. One night a divinely inspired thought occurred—request an MBO for a good night's sleep. I fell asleep almost immediately and slept though the night. I repeated the experiment with the same results. Thank you for the inspiration."

Thanks Julie. That's a benevolent outcome request I hadn't thought of.

REQUEST ASSISTANCE IN SPIRITUAL GROWTH

Kelly writes: "I wanted to share with you a new recent use of MBO requests that I've employed. I regularly consult oracle cards of various types, and one of my favorites is Doreen Virtue's *Daily Guidance from Your Angels* deck. When I pull a card and read the guidance, I request an MBO for assistance following through as suggested. This is especially helpful when it may be an emotionally challenging suggestion. I have noticed that I again feel my companions in spirit are helping me out, as I bring thoughts of the oracle guidance to my awareness throughout my day—knowing I have assistance/ company sure helps, even if it is just as a frame of reference.

"As a result, I feel I am more successful following the suggested guidance offered to me. I know I haven't given specifics on the guidance, but I think I've made my point. So as I see it, the requests for MBOs can assist in one's spiritual growth in this way too. Thanks so much for your great work."

<hr />

Notice how requesting benevolent outcomes makes you more aware and heightens your sensitivity while raising your vibrations.

In the Garden

Karin in Ontario writes: "I would like to share my recent experience with an MBO. Two weeks ago, I wanted to trim tree branches in my garden. These were very low branches but of many different sizes. Being alone at the time, I mustered the courage to sever a branch approximately one inch in diameter by myself. Well, I just did not have the strength in my arms to cut this branch, so I paused and requested an MBO for help. I waited about two minutes or so, then tried again. This time my shears were like cutting through butter. I was pleased and amazed at this. Thank you for your help."

In the Kitchen

Annette writes: "I've been reading your book *The Gentle Way* and first of all I want to thank you for writing it and secondly, for writing it in a way that is simple to use and understand. I've had some interesting results. The best was finding an item that a friend of my husband broke—he is staying with us temporarily. The pan has not been made in over twenty years and it was something I used for a specific kind of cooking. When I went to the manufacturer's website to see if I could order a replacement, it was over sixty dollars. I requested an MBO to find a reasonable replacement and I found one that was like new on www.ebay.com. I bid $20.00 and won it for $14.95. With shipping, it came to $28.97.

"Then I found the other item on ebay, a Tupperware colander that this same friend accidentally melted. It is made with holes only in the bottom and it fits with my other containers perfectly—and this colander hasn't been made in close to thirty years. I was able to get it with shipping for $18.50. I didn't even ask for that—outcome, but since I was trying to replace items I often used as a set, my guardian angel put me in touch with how to replace them both! They are both like they've never been used! And the person who damaged them gave me the money for them, plus extra toward utilities.

"Since I am new to requesting MBOs, I was wondering how to go about asking for something to continue to function and not break down, at least until I am financially in a place to repair or replace said item. For example, our hot water heater was installed nine years ago. The warranty expired three years ago and yesterday we noticed the spigot was dripping. Would I request an MBO for our hot water heater to continue to work until we are more financially stable? Should I request that all our appliances and equipment continue to function while we go through this rough patch? Does it matter how I word the MBO? I want to make certain that my intent is presented properly."

"I have read through a third of your book, taking breaks periodically to digest the information and understand it. It is all new to me, talking to my angel for things, but it makes more sense each day. I have looked through the book and did not see a request relating to asking that something work longer instead of for easily finding a person to repair it, but I may have overlooked this."

⟫-◦-⟪

You're right. That's one of the things that's not in the first book, but it is touched on in the second book! You do have a couple of MBOs you can request, and you can do both:

> *Most Benevolent Outcome*
>
> *"I request a most benevolent outcome that the water heater continue to work properly until I can afford to replace it, thank you."*

Or ask for an MBO for a replacement that you can afford, and see what your guardian angel comes up with. You can always add the tagline "and may it be even better than I hope for or expect, thank you!"

What about checking craigslist in your area? Sometimes people want a specific type of water heater and replace one that still has a lot of life left in it—we did when we bought our house. That could be a good interim solution. Sometimes a plumber, who might need some side work, might either offer you one, or might keep an eye out for one for you for the cost of, say, a hundred dollars plus labor. The plumbing companies would not want to do this, though, as there's probably not enough profit in there for them.

And one more thing: I would suggest keeping your friend out of the kitchen—he sounds like a walking accident, probably because he is concerned about his situation.

Annette wrote to update me: "I did the MBO for the hot water heater and for paying down my bills. Friday, when I talked to the credit union about lowering my payments on our cars, I was told if I refinanced, we could get a lower interest rate. Then the loan officer asked me if I knew we had equity in my husband's car. We could get that money we refinanced—about $3,000.

"Tuesday, the day after Memorial Day, the credit union called and said it was all approved—we had over $4,000 in equity they would deposit in our account once we signed the papers. I went home to a letter from my mom. As I was putting my finger in the envelope to open it, she called, and as I was talking with her I opened it to find a check for $750. She said she wanted to make certain we could replace the hot water heater and that she intended to write it for $150 but wrote a seven accidentally and decided to just write it for $750. Normally I would have felt horrible for my Mom to send me money, but I didn't ask her, and I knew my guardian angel and hers had worked together so I could get the hot water heater. That way Mom, who is eighty-eight, would not be eight hundred miles away worrying about my hot water heater. I've also been guided to information on a nonprofit credit counseling service just a few blocks up the street that is listed with an A-plus rating from the Better Business Bureau. Thank you, thank you, thank you my guardian angel!"

My wife Dena has been working on the kitchen in our new house. The pullout drawers for dishes did not have cutouts at the back like the ones in our old house did, which prevented two sets of dishes being stored inside them.

She marked the cutouts for our daughter to remove with her electric saw, but marked the wrong ends—and with permanent marker! Well, she is happy to report that she requested a benevolent outcome to remove the marks with Bon Ami and it worked—they came right off! She was afraid she was going to have to live with them marked up in the front.

CHAPTER THREE

BENEVOLENT OUTCOMES FOR YOUR FINANCES

E veryone goes through ups and downs with personal finances. Here are some great stories of people who requested MBOs for their financial problems.

Bev writes: "I've been reading your column in the *Sedona Journal of Emergence!* for some time but recently had occasion to really put the MBO to the test. I received a letter from the IRS saying I was going to owe about $8,000 because of an error in 2006. I immediately requested an MBO. I talked to my accountant this morning, and rather than paying the $8,000, I'm going to get a refund for $2,000 from my federal taxes, as well as a refund from the state. It doesn't get any better than that. I'm encouraging my friends to use MBOs too."

REFINANCING AND CREDIT CARDS

Renee in Nevada writes: "I have been using MBOs ever since I read your first article. I'm very grateful and blessed with these experiences, but I just have to relay this particular one to you and your readers. My astrologer told me in February that we should refinance our house by June of this year, because he did a chart on the U.S. economy and it was not going to be favorable, to say the least, after that time. Even though we had until December to refinance, it was hard to give up our 4.25 percent mortgage rate, and we knew we were going to pay more than that. So I put out an MBO for our refinance and was thinking we probably would be paying at least $500 more a month.

"Well, to make a long story shorter, we ended up with a payment that was $20 less a month than our original mortgage payment, and we expected to get about $3,300 back from this refinance. Much to our amazement, when escrow closed, we got back almost $11,000. Now that surpassed all my expectations for an MBO. Thanks so much for enlightening your readers about MBOs. They truly work wonders and blessings."

Deb writes: "Hi, Tom. I had such a great MBO this week; I couldn't wait to share it with you. I have two credit card accounts and I hadn't been able to pay on them. I was looking at almost $500 on one and $300 on the other one. I was so stressed that I decided to call them and see if I could lower my payment. I explained why I couldn't pay—I didn't have the money. I talked to two of the nicest people I have ever dealt with. On both accounts they lowered the payments—$150 to $50 on one and $69 on the other. They also cancelled all of the late fees and interest. Every penny is going toward paying the accounts off. This was the result of my practicing MBOs. I was ecstatic—I felt like a weight lifted off of me. Bless you, Tom, for introducing me to MBOs. Have a blessed week."

Preferred Banking

Patricia in British Columbia writes: "Since I last contacted you, I have had many wonderful MBO results. I do the affirmations and prayers you gave us on a regular basis. The latest results: I declared bankruptcy thirteen years ago, and since then have been turned down for credit on a regular basis, because I have no credit history. When I went to my bank last week to make a deposit, I asked for an MBO that I would not have too long to stand in the line, as I have osteoarthritis in my knees and cannot walk or stand for more than a few minutes. As always now, I don't even have to ask for a parking space at the door, as this automatically happens.

"The bank manager (a relatively new one) met me and asked if I would prefer to sit at one of the cubicles and have someone come to me. I thanked him, and he proceeded to serve me himself. During the course of the transaction, he asked me if I had a credit card. I said that I did not and told him of the bankruptcy and of my history of trying for credit. He then asked me if I would like a Visa. I immediately thought, 'Here we go again,' and said (not too enthusiastically) that it would be nice. His next words were, 'It is done; you will have your card in ten days, delivered to your door.' Well, it happened! I received a notice saying I was accepted, and then the card arrived. To me, this is a miracle, as I'm seventy-three years old and living on a government pension. I cannot thank you enough for the information on MBOs, and I will send one to Oprah. I have had so many on a daily basis.

"Here is one more quickie: We have been having a heat wave with temperatures of 100 degrees and over. I cannot take prolonged heat like this and was getting ill. I asked for an

MBO to have the temperature in my house lowered to a more comfortable temperature, and lo and behold: that night it was cooler in the house, so I could sleep. The next day, it was 70 degrees indoors the whole day, and the temperature has stayed that comfortable ever since. I spend most of my days giving thanks. Amazing!"

For Paying Bills and Debt Forgiveness

Bernadette writes: "Tom, I am enjoying all the newsletters. Can you give me an affirmation that I can write on my bills when they arrive? It would be much appreciated."

———◦———

Well, to Bernadette and to everyone, one thing I do each month is to request an MBO for being able to pay all our bills for that month. As an example you could say:

Most Benevolent Outcome
> "I request an MBO for paying all the bills that will come due in the month of November, thank you!"

For some specific bills, such as electricity, you could say:

Most Benevolent Outcome
> "I request an MBO to find ways to reduce my monthly electric bill, thank you!"

You could request the same MBO for gas, water and heating oil, depending upon what part of the country you're in.

Stefanye from Texas writes: "I've been using MBOs for a few weeks now and have seen all sorts of positive things happen. In addition to great parking spaces, zipping through traffic and getting great service at restaurants, I had one MBO that was pretty amazing.

"A few years ago, I became disabled and was unable to pay my bills. It was months before I was approved for disability and started getting a small monthly check plus food stamps, and by the time money started coming in again, the penalties and interest were so high on my credit cards that I'd never be able to catch them up, much less get them paid off.

"After months and months of harassment, the credit card companies finally 'forgave' my debts and wrote them off—all but one. In Texas, the statute of limitations is four years. The remaining creditor waited three years and eleven months, and then filed suit against me. To make a long story short, we went to court last month, but I didn't realize I was supposed to bring in paperwork. The judge gave me thirty days. I kept asking for MBOs regarding this lawsuit. I also communicate with angels, and the response they gave me when I asked what the outcome would be was, 'It will all work out according to your highest good. Do not fret.'

"I continued to pray for MBOs regarding this case, and the day before I was to go to court, a very nice clerk from the law firm that was suing me called and said that they had decided 'not to pursue this case any further.' She gave me the local number so that I could confirm with the courthouse. I called and talked to a clerk at the courthouse and she said, 'For some strange reason, they've decided to drop the lawsuit. I just don't understand it. This doesn't usually happen.' They could have easily gotten a judgment against me and it was pretty much a slam-dunk case, according to a friend of mine who is an attorney. So when they dropped it, well, I believe it was due to an MBO."

ON HOME OWNERSHIP

Diane in Dallas writes: "Today I was told I could not have my home loan. I prayed for an MBO and a couple hours later, I got a second letter from the realtor. I got the loan and am finally going to own a home! At 4:11 PM they told me the bad news, but by 6:26 PM they had fixed it, and I am closing!"

⇒⇒-◦-◄⊏

[Diane referenced an email sent to her denying her loan and requiring her to provide all sorts of extra financial information. Then she received the following message from another person at the Texas lending institution she had applied to]:

"We have fixed it. I have a migraine now; we scrambled and we got this done. It was a miracle. I can't believe it!"

Charlene writes: "I'd like to second Diane's MBO outcome on buying a house. It does work. I first found out about you and MBOs last July when it seemed totally hopeless that I could ever own my own home. I started using the prayer right away and signed the paperwork for my home in September of 2008! I'd say a couple months is a great turnaround time for a miracle. Thank you for the light you bring to the world!"

⇒⇒-◦-◄⊏

And thank you, Charlene, for sharing such positive news!

STRESSED AND DEPRESSED

Diane writes: "How do you say an MBO for a person you love who suffers from depression and is stressed out? It seems a lot of people get stressed out over things like bills, money and so on. So how do we handle it ourselves to keep balanced, and how do we request our angels to help the other person? Need a little guidance here. Thank you—always expecting great things!"

———

You can say, "I ask that any and all beings send massive amounts of loving energy and pink light to _____, who is stressed and depressed, and assist him/her to feel better about himself/herself and know he/she can contribute to society too, thank you!" There are other, different benevolent prayers you can make up yourself to say on other days that will pertain to their specific situation.

CHAPTER FOUR

BENEVOLENT OUTCOMES FOR YOUR VEHICLE

M any people spend a portion of their day in their cars—commuting to and from work, doing errands, attending events and parties, and so forth. I received a number of stories about these trips. Be sure that each time you're traveling from point A to B—or B to C, and yes, even C to D—you request a benevolent outcome for your drive there. I request MBOs for each part of my daily drive.

Clara wrote: "I used an MBO a week ago for a 200-mile round-trip freeway trip. The freeway is always crowded at that time, but it was not for us. It was amazing. My grandson was driving, and he kept saying, 'Where is everybody?' It was smooth sailing. I had to do that same trip this weekend, but I forgot to 'request' until we were on the freeway in heavy traffic, so I asked the angels, if it wasn't too late, would they please help out? Oh Tom, here is the amazing part—it was like they were parting the traffic for us. Although it was heavy, we were traveling as if we had the freeway to ourselves. We were not held up anywhere, but more amazingly, we just missed a twenty-three-car crash, and we were guided right past a big trailer that had blown a wheel and was throwing heavy sparks. All of these things the angels did for me make me feel so loved and cared for. I feel peaceful and very happy!"

——⊷•⊶——

Then Clara wrote again to give me some good news. She had requested a benevolent outcome for receiving a financial settlement that had been due her for quite some time. She had been unable to buy a car for a long time, and the financial settlement gave her the ability to purchase one. She requested an MBO for a car to meet her needs and even more. Clara visualized a car driven by a little old lady, something that she no longer drove but that was still in good condition. Her son brought her a list of five cars that appeared on craigslist for her area. One of the five was just perfect. An elderly lady had passed away, leaving her 2000 model car with only 41,000 miles. It had a leather interior with all the bells and whistles. Clara had requested the perfect car for herself, and her guardian angel arranged, through her son, for her to find it! She added that she now needs to find a better house, and of course she says that she can hardly wait to see what her guardian angel will find for her when she requests that perfect house!

BENEVOLENT OUTCOME DELAY

Harry in Texas writes: "I was scheduled to drive my step-dad from Mt. Pleasant, Texas, to Tyler on Tuesday, May 6, for eye surgery. On Monday, May 5, I drove to Red Oak, Texas, to the Shooting Star Ranch and Retreat to take pictures of a site location for a labyrinth our group wishes to build. I also took all my massage equipment so I could give the owner of the retreat a massage.

"I asked for an MBO for the trip, and when I got there and stopped to open the horse gate to let myself in, my car transmission only buzzed when I put it in drive to move through the gate. I tried several times with the same loud buzzing. Then I pulled the gearshift to low gear and the car moved forward slowly through the gate. I stopped, got out and closed the gate, continuing on to the house in low gear. As a woman came out to see who was there, I told her what had happened. Then I said: 'And I asked for a most benevolent outcome for this trip today.'

"To make a long story shorter, I had a tow truck come and take the car to the transmission garage in Garland near where I live and made arrangements with my son to come pick me up that afternoon with all my massage equipment. When I got back home later that afternoon, I contacted my stepdad to let him know what had happened, and to see what time I had to be there the next morning to get him to his appointment on time. His appointment was at 7:45 AM. This meant that I would have to leave my home at 4:00 AM to pick him up in Mt. Pleasant by 6:00 AM so we could leave at 6:15 AM for Tyler.

"Then it hit me—here was my MBO! If I had not traveled to Red Oak that morning, if I'd just stayed home and left for Mt. Pleasant the next morning, there was a good chance that my transmission would have broken somewhere between Greenville and Sulphur Springs on IH-30 around 4:30 AM in the middle of nowhere. Then I would have been in a panic to contact my stepdad that early in the morning and have him find someone else on such short notice to take him to Tyler. Also, I would have had to wait until daylight to get my car problem corrected.

"As it was morning, panic mode didn't set in, and emergency procedures were handled expeditiously. I had the car in the shop by noon and didn't get it back until Friday. My younger sister took the day off and drove our stepdad to Tyler in my place. Sometimes MBOs are blessings disguised as difficult problems, but they are indeed blessings, because they avert other, more difficult situations."

⸺❈⸺

I couldn't have said it better myself, Harry!

You Have to Make the Request!

Kelly wrote: "I have been asking for benevolent outcomes for my arrival to work. My drive has gone from an hour to thirty or forty minutes. On Monday I forgot to ask for an MBO on my way to work, and it took me over an hour to get there.

"The first day that I asked for an MBO, I heard a voice in my head reminding me to take a different route because the other on-ramp to the freeway was closed. And on the day when I forgot to ask for one, I started to take my old route, and it took me over an hour to get to work."

Rain and Parking Woes

Gail writes: "I have received many benevolent outcomes since reading your book, but one I received the other day was unusual. I parked in a parking lot at my church. When I got back to my car after the service, someone had pulled in two inches from my car on the driver's side. I tried to back out but got even closer, and even touched the other car. I kind of freaked out a little and started to get angry, but I actively told myself not to get angry about it, calmed myself some and requested a benevolent outcome. What happened next was really a miracle. I tried a second time to get out and it was as if the cars had moved—they seemed four inches from each other and I got out with no problem. If I hadn't been there, I wouldn't have believed it!"

Julie writes: "I had a most amazing MBO yesterday. I was going to a new metaphysical group. I live in a semi-rural area and this group meets at a coffee shop forty-four miles away, pretty much in the city of St. Louis. I had never been at this coffee shop before. It was a pretty long way to go. First of all, we were supposed to have rain all weekend, and it was raining hard in the morning. I asked for an MBO to not have rain to prevent us all from getting soaked. Right before I left, though there were still dark clouds, it stopped raining and there was just a really fine sprinkle off and on. The Sun even came out through the dark clouds. It was amazing.

"When I got there, it was a little bitty coffee shop on the corner of two major streets with very little parallel parking on the street. I hate to parallel park. There was none available, so I went down and through an alley around the block and asked for an MBO, (though I didn't think it was possible) for a great parking space that I could just pull into without having to parallel park. On my second pass, there was the perfect place, one car back from right in front, which was probably like a space and a half, and I was able to just pull in and then back up a little. I was totally amazed! Thanks so much for all your teachings on MBOs."

FOR POOR WEATHER CONDITIONS

Renee from Lake Tahoe writes: "I want to share with you what happened to me a couple of months ago. We had our first snow day about the second week of October, and I had a doctor's appointment in Reno that day. To travel from Lake Tahoe to Reno, you must go over a very winding mountain pass at an elevation of approximately 8,900 feet. Before I left, I said an MBO for a safe roundtrip.

"On the way back over the mountain pass from Reno, it started snowing a little bit harder. Right when I thought I should put my car in four-wheel drive, I lost control of my vehicle and spun around through the oncoming lane and into the embankment on the other side of the road, facing down the mountain. Fortunately, there was no oncoming traffic, so I did not hit anyone else. Needless to say, I was quite shaken, though not hurt. I quickly headed down the mountain until I could pull over to investigate the damage. As I got out of my car, a man and his son pulled over and asked me if I was okay, because they'd been driving by just as it happened. My car was banged up on the bumper and missing the grill. He said to wait for him there; he was going back up to see if he could recover the missing parts.

"As I waited for him, a big semi-trailer truck pulled over beside me and let at least a dozen or more cars go by. Shortly after that, the man came back with my grill and told me how lucky I was not to have been involved in that mess of the truck and cars. I knew then that my MBO for a safe trip had kept me from further harm. I felt very blessed. So it goes to show you, if I hadn't asked for an MBO, things could have been much worse."

Remember, folks: You're still going to have challenges and adventures in your lives. Otherwise, things would be awfully dull. But requesting MBOs keeps the challenges within reason.

Twanda in Michigan writes: "I would like to tell you about this MBO. It was this past Friday, December 19. I live in Michigan and we were hit with a big snowstorm. So I'm trying to go to the store, and as I was trying to enter the driveway of the grocery store, I got stuck in the snow. No going forward or backward. So I asked for an MEO for getting unstuck.

"I sat there for five to six minutes blocking two lanes of the road, when up came a lady who proceeded to try and push my car out. It didn't budge. I told her, "Thanks, but I'll just wait for a police cruiser." She said, "I'll push again with the help of this man who's approaching." They got me out in two seconds. I never saw her coming, or the man. Thank you so much for introducing me to MBOs."

⸻⸺◦⸻⸺

I think Twanda's guardian angel was doing a little overtime work for her.

Joy writes: "My daughter and I went to a funeral in Minnesota the first weekend in May. It was mostly uneventful and we actually enjoyed going, as we were able to visit with many relatives. We stayed with my sister, who lives 90 miles north of Minneapolis.

"On our return trip home we had to leave her place at 2:30 AM to catch our flight at 6:00 AM. There was a slight rain when we started out, but within five miles, we were driving through a cloudburst. I could feel our SUV hydroplane. I asked for an

MBO; I had forgotten to ask earlier. The rain almost immediately slackened and within a few miles we were driving on almost dry road. I'm sure they knew the request was coming and were anxious to get started."

Rick wrote: "Every day before I go to work, I request an MBO to arrive safely at work and in a timely fashion. I work in the Wachovia Center, the home arena of the Philadelphia Flyers and 76ers. The Flyers played a day game yesterday, and I worked earlier than scheduled. Parking down there is a nightmare for Flyers games. I expected to have to park somewhere far away, just short of a small cab ride.

"I added to my daily MBO that I would have a parking space available to me close to the front door to our office. Sure enough, a ten-minute ride through the parking lot, looking for a space was reduced to thirty seconds; there were three spots within several feet of each other available to me. They weren't close to the front door, but they were in an area where we're supposed to park on game days (our normal parking spaces in the arena parking lot are reserved for season-ticket holders on game day). To top it off, I left work last night requesting an MBO for green traffic lights on the way home, and every light was green."

FINDING A NEW CAR

Stefanye writes: "Here's one that happened to my mother. She doesn't really know about MBOs, but I've been saying them for her. On September 11 of this year, a drunk driver hit her, and her 1995 Avalon was totaled. Miraculously, she only suffered some bruising and whiplash. She ended up receiving $5,800 for her car. She's almost eighty and on a fixed income. I continually asked for MBOs for her so she could find the perfect car for her. In the meantime, I've been using my car to drive her to physical therapy, grocery shopping and so on.

"I don't know if this was prophetic on my part, but I kept encouraging her and told her that I had asked angels to assist in finding her a car. People were giving her advice right and left about how she should get a little puddle-jumper, how she wouldn't get much with $5,800 and the like. I told her I felt like there was a fantastic car—like a Lincoln or a Cadillac—sitting in some little old lady's garage that she would be thrilled with and that practically had her name on it. I told her that little lady would not be able to drive any more and that her family would practically give it away. My mother was skeptical for sure, but I kept encouraging her and kept asking for MBOs.

"One day, my sister was visiting from Seattle and she was browsing through the local paper. She saw an ad for a 2004 Silver Signature Lincoln Town Car. The lady's husband had died and she'd had a stroke and couldn't drive anymore. They wanted $11,000, which was actually below Blue Book value. The original price of the car was $35,000. Her brother-in-law had just put new tires on it. It was like brand new. That week we had just gotten our insurance check from the damages of Hurricane Ike, so she had extra cash in the bank and in a couple of months would be getting her check compensating for the pain and suffering due to the accident, and she would be able to finish with any repairs that might still need to be made.

"We called and left a message and when her brother-in-law called back, he said he'd had several calls, but since ours was first, he would wait and let us decide. Of course, we bought the car. The synchronicity of all this is, I believe, due to the MBO I had asked for.

"To say that she's excited is an understatement, and I am too! It is so thrilling to have what I call a 'spiritual tool' in the form of MBOs. I can't thank you enough for making the information available. I've communicated directly with angels for years, but asking for MBOs is so much more powerful. And remember the commercial about the rotisserie cooker? The one where you can just 'set it and forget it'? Well, I feel the same way with MBOs. I can just ask for what I want or need and then let the angels do the driving—or cooking, so to speak."

Flat Tires

Dawn writes: "I would like to share my MBO—here it goes. I had an eye doctor appointment today at 4:30 PM. The office called and asked if I could come in at 2:30 PM because they had a cancellation. At 2:00 PM I left work and started driving to my appointment. After a few moments, I felt that I had a flat tire and requested my first MBO.

"I pulled over to see how bad it was. It was indeed flat. I slowly moved to a nearby shopping center to park, because I could not leave my car where it was. Next, I called a lady at work and asked her to either take me to my doctor's appointment or to please let me borrow her car for a few minutes. She said, "I will come and get you." She drove me and, how wonderful, I was there at exactly 2:30 PM. The doctor said it was the fastest procedure she'd ever done.

"We came back to change my tire and put the donut on. I have never had to change a tire on my Jeep. I found my jack and tools rusted and hard to manage, so I put another MBO in place. Two men came by immediately and changed my tire. One of the men told me my spare was very low and I would need to get air as soon as possible. I did not make it out of the parking lot. I decided to walk back to work since my car had not gotten very far from work earlier.

"A second lady I work with saw me walking. She pulled over and when I explained the situation she said, "I have Fix-a-Flat." We went to my car. The donut was off the rim and we had to remove the spare and use the can on the original tire. That's when I said my third MBO. Immediately another two men took over the tire adventure. They found a large chunk of ceramic deep in the tire, removed it, plugged the hole and filled the tire with fix-a-flat. One of the two men who'd helped me used to work on tires and always carried plugging tools with him. They followed me to the gas station for air. This all took place within two hours. Wow!"

Notice that Dawn requested a benevolent outcome when the problem first occurred, which set up all the other benevolent outcomes, resulting in the final MBO!

CAR REPAIR

Norine in Rochester, New York, writes: "A couple months ago, a friend of mine in Arizona told me about you and your book. Now, I was brought up in your typical Italian-American family, and we believed in angels and guardian angels, that things happen for a reason, that you should just trust things to work out for the best and so on. So my initial conversation with my friend resonated as truth with me. Even though I no longer follow Catholicism, I kept some of the things I still believed in, which included angels. My cat's name is even Angelica!

"Over the years I have had many miraculous happenings. I have often said that my guardian angel must want to put in for a job change because of all the difficult situations she's helped me out with. So why would I even buy or read your book? I mean you'd be preaching to the choir, because I already have my experiences, right?

"Well, here's the deal . . . I was never taught that I could ask my guardian angel for things. I just thought guardian angels were there, on call, if you will, and would show up when necessary. It's kind of odd now that I think about, because I was taught you could pray to saints and your prayers would be answered; you could pray to the Blessed Mother, and it would be ditto on the prayers answered thing, but no one ever suggested you could do that with a guardian angel. After a while you almost forget they are there for you unless some lifesaving thing comes up. So thank you. You showed me that I was under utilizing my guardian angel. I could ask for things and they didn't even have to be big, important things. So here's the story of the benevolent outcome—actually, two.

"I know you said to start with a small request, but the day I learned about requesting MBOs I actually had a big thing, so I thought, why not? Back in late summer, my car's anti lock braking system (ABS) light came on and it started to make an odd noise. My mechanic told me a sensor had defaulted and the ABS wouldn't work. Since it was an expensive proposition to fix, I asked if I could hold off on repairs. He said I could but that when winter came (I live where we get a lot of snow); I should get it fixed, for obvious safety reasons.

"November came and so did the snow. I had an appointment to get my snow tires on, and he said it really was time to fix the ABS. Quite honestly, the cost was a bit prohibitive at that particular time, but I scheduled it anyway, thinking the money would come. The night before my appointment, which is when I found out about MBOs, I requested a benevolent outcome so that I would be safe, even if I decided not to do the ABS repair (I would just rely on pumping brakes if needed, like we did in the old days) and asked for the outcome to be better than what I could even anticipate.

"Well, the next morning, I got in my car and the ABS light wasn't on and the noise was gone! I brought it into the shop and nothing was wrong with the ABS, so I just had the snow tires put on. It's now been about two months and all is still well with the car. Wow! Who knew my guardian angel knew car mechanics? Boy, have I ever said thank you, thank you, thank you!"

Tresta writes: "I have been constantly disciplining myself to request my MBOs. I recently had an incident with my car. On this particular morning, I dropped my children off to school. After that I went to the gas station and headed home. Mind you, I live on an island (St. Thomas, Virgin Island). If you've ever been there, you would know that it is very mountainous.

"Back to the story. I was driving up the side of the hill, and I veered to the right. I noticed I was veering a little too far to the right. I steered right back to my lane and stopped the car. I got out, looked under the car and didn't see anything loose. I quickly got on the phone to my husband and informed him what was going on. I told him to stay on the phone with me as I put the car in second gear, turned the hazard lights on and drove slowly home. Before I took off, I immediately said my MBO: 'I request a most benevolent outcome for this car to arrive safely at home.' What do you know? I made it safely! My husband called the mechanic, who came out, looked at the car and called me over.

"We both looked under the car. To my surprise, he showed me that the steering rod was completely off the wheel. He asked how I made it home. I immediately said, 'My guardian angels.' Once again, thank you, Tom."

Six Thousand Miles of MBOs

Karen writes: "In February, I had been on disability for a while, and the need to see my only grandchild, a grandson, became almost unbearable. His home is about 2,300 miles away. I have an old dog who is a wonderful traveling companion and she was welcome at my daughter's home, so I loaded up my Saturn Vue and off we went. When we got headed to connect with Highway 40, I made my request of an MBO for our trip.

"I am in my sixty-eighth year and love to travel, especially drive, so the trip was exciting for me. I was confronted with ice and snow but fared well—we got snow-stranded in Kingman, Arizona, so I took a U-turn and went through Havasu City. I spied the London Bridge and saw some of the most breathtaking sites along the Colorado River!

"I had been having a fuel tank thing with my car and I gassed up at intervals of 150 to 200 miles to be sure I wouldn't run out of gas in support of the MBOs for my car running well. As we went along, I was led to gas stations whose existence I never would have guessed. It took me a whole day to drive across Texas, from El Paso to Shreveport, and MBOs kept me alert and enjoying the drive. I saw areas I never dreamed I would and enjoyed every inch of them.

"While visiting my grandson, my Vue failed and I traded it in for a new car after requesting an MBO. I had possession of the new car with all the papers signed and such and drove to Virginia and back for a one-day excursion. The deal on the new car fell through the next day, so I was back with the Vue. I got repair help to get it well enough to drive back home, thanks to my MBO and my son-in-law.

"I am grateful for the lesson of using MBOs. I took this nearly 6,000-mile round trip and saw new states to add to my goal of seeing all of the lower 48, and didn't suffer. My Vue was having ailments and couldn't face going to Virginia, so because of my MBO I was given a new car to drive there! And my Vue made the trip back to my home just fine!"

Brakes

Teddy from Maryland writes: "I was having trouble with squeaking brakes that finally turned into a horrible metal scraping sound. I'm more of a books and theory sort of guy and am not very mechanically inclined, so I had no idea what was going on, just that something was wrong with the brakes.

"I took my car to a major brake and muffler chain and asked for an MBO that repairs to the brakes cost $200 or less, as that was about all I could afford at the time. I got a call back later that day from the shop and was told it would be $700 to replace the brake pads and rotors. I thanked them but told them I could not pay that right now. I made arrangements to pick up the car that evening. I was disappointed that my prayer had not been answered but then remembered to just have faith and let the spirit guides do their work as they saw fit.

"I had borrowed my brother's truck to run stock I was selling in a show, and as we made plans to return the truck, I told him what was going on and the amount the chain had given me for an estimate. He agreed that it sounded a bit high and said he might be able to replace the parts in a few weeks. He told me to call a few auto parts stores and told me what parts to ask about. I was very surprised to find out that the needed parts were readily available and all for about $180!

"I picked him up after work and he drove me over to pick up my car. I was not looking forward to driving my car for the next two weeks with the metal-on-metal sound every time I had to stop, but I thought waiting was better than paying $700. When we got to where the car was, my brother agreed to drive my car directly home while I picked up the parts in his truck so I'd have them when he was ready to replace them.

"When I finally got home with the parts, my brother had already gathered the tools necessary and said my car was so bad he was not going to let me drive it another week with no brake pads. He got to work on them right away. He proceeded to change the pads and the rotors in my driveway in less than twenty minutes! I was amazed at how quickly and easily he did the repair and very pleased with the cost also. I had received my requested MBO: better than I had expected!"

PARKING

Arlena writes: "I requested an MBO for my niece. Where my mother lives, the parking is very bad. I requested the MBO in front of my sister, and I left her looking out the window. I went to the family room, and when she called me, I asked her what she wanted. She asked me what I'd said about the parking, and I told her I'd requested a most benevolent outcome that Melinda find a parking place in front of my mother's building. She did park in front of the building. The angels are always there. Thank you."

CHAPTER FIVE

BENEVOLENT OUTCOMES FOR FAMILY AND FRIENDS

Recently here in Dallas my son could not find his very expensive cell phone—to call it just a cell phone does not do it justice. He looked all over his bedroom and office in our house and then looked in his car and so on. Naturally, he called his cell phone from all over the house but couldn't find it. I reminded him to request a benevolent outcome, and he did.

My wife asked me to search his car once again, so I took my cell phone to ring his, along with a flashlight. When I rang it and heard no sound, I said out loud to myself, "It's not here." After it went to voice message, I dialed again and as it rang, my son came up behind me with his cell phone ringing. It had been buried in a drawer in his desk, and for some reason, he didn't hear it ringing before. I got to go back to my television after eleven hours in the office. A nice, quick MBO!

Charlene writes: "When I write out my MBOs, I put them on flashcards and post them where I can see and read them easily all day long. The first time I write an MBO out, I do say it out loud, but then I simply read the words after that. I don't change the words, I simply wait. Once the MBO has become a reality, I take the card down.

"You say the request only has to be made once and that it must be changed out every day. Sorry, but that confuses me. Am I going about this all wrong? I've been granted everything I've asked for very quickly using the flashcards—longest wait was three months, so I find it hard to believe I'm doing this wrong. Help?

"The other strange thing that's going on is even though I've told my partner and my sister about MBOs and they say they've tried with no results, when I create an MBO for them for their requests, things start happening for them very quickly. Why is that?"

————◦————

I think it's fine to post the cards, as it is a mental reminder that you requested the MBO. I think it helps create the event—junior creator in training. You're expecting it to happen! And elsewhere you'll read that Theo says it's okay to repeat an MBO request.

I find that when people say they have requested MBOs and they "don't work," it's either because they requested something so far off it doesn't seem to have been successful, or they really are rejecting it but want to tell you they tried. They might be lazy—after all, this takes a little concentration to make it a habit—or they can't believe, because of previous religious training, that people can actually make these requests and they'll be answered. Many people have been taught that they're "not worthy," that only some religious leader can make requests for them.

When you request an MBO in front of such people and it happens, then it will remind them that this actually works—

especially if it is something simple like a parking spot or any of the mundane things we do every day. Remember, as I wrote about in the book, there is a radiant effect, so when you request an MBO for yourself, it can include others too. If it's just for others, you're supposed to say, "I ask _____" in the form of a benevolent prayer, as a whole different set of angels handle those requests instantly.

FOR SOLDIERS

Rhavda writes: "Your newsletter is wonderful and a great accompaniment to your book. I have been working with MBOs since last March, and this Christmas I have given away ten copes of your book to friends who needed to work with MBOs. My question for you is, do you have any MBOs that we can use for our military people who are stationed around the world? This Christmas I gave a copy of your book to my son, who is a Marine, but I feel I need to give him something shorter that he can use, something that will catch his attention. Our soldiers need this type of inspirational information to help them through their darkest hours."

Here's what I've suggested in the past for those serving in war zones to request (and I know it worked, at least with one Marine I was given information about):

Most Benevolent Outcome
"I request a most benevolent outcome for my drive
(trip, and so on) to _____, thank you!"

Most Benevolent Outcome
"I request a most benevolent outcome for my return
from this patrol safely, thank you!"

The request must be benevolent for all those involved in the request, so it would not work, for example, if he requested an MBO for killing someone before they killed him, for instance. What actually would happen with the ones I gave above is that if he's on a patrol, the bad guys might have just left that area, gone to eat, been called back by their commander or whatever. He comes back safe, but with no negative actions or repercussions. It is truly a benevolent outcome for everyone.

It also has what I call in the first book the "radiant effect," as those close by normally are in that bubble of energy surrounding the person who requested the MBO. It might be a boring tour of duty, but he doesn't pick up any karma that has to be balanced later, in this life or any other. That's why I had to experience congestive heart failure in this lifetime, as Theo explained; I had killed some people in a war in another life and brought heartache to their families and friends, so I had to physically experience heartache this time around to balance the scales. Your son can also say a benevolent prayer for his comrades:

Benevolent Prayer
"I ask that any and all beings assist and aid us in safely
reaching _____, thank you!"

Benevolent Prayer
"I ask that any and all beings assist and aid us in
returning safely from this patrol, thank you!"

Remember, his guardian angel handles the MBO requests and a whole set of whole souls that we call angels instantly responds to the benevolent prayers. Theo says there are a little over a million of these souls handling all types of prayers around the world. They're great multitaskers.

What Children Think

Diane in the UK writes: "Here is a delightful MBO story that thrilled me because it involves my seven-year-old niece, Jessica.

"I bought *The Gentle Way* as a Christmas gift for my beautiful sister-in-law, Tracy, who has been having wonderful MBO successes. The other morning, busy mom Tracy asked for an MBO for a parking space near the kids' school. Running a little late and becoming agitated with the rush hour traffic, Tracy again asked for an MBO for a parking space. Jessica spoke up, 'You know what's going to happen now? You're gonna get two spaces!' And as Tracy said, 'We did. That's exactly what happened. There were two spaces, one in front of the other where normally you are hard pressed to find one.' How funny!

"One of the best parts about the story for me is that beautiful little Jess is trusting, by example from her Mom, how to live and ask for MBOs. Wonderful!"

Bernadette writes: "I have been saying my affirmation each morning, and I must say I am a great believer. I have received money, my hair stylist did my hair free and I went into JCPenny to get a blanket and when I got to the cashier, my friend paid for it.

"This is the one that made me a great believer, though. My grandson had to give a speech for his exam. I told him to request a most benevolent outcome for a good grade, and we did it together. A few weeks later he called to say he'd gotten an A. I said thank you. I am happy now, for each day I expect great things."

CHILD CUSTODY

Angela writes: "Please explain the benevolent prayer. I wondered about prayer for a benevolent outcome for someone else. I need a benevolent prayer for my son and granddaughter. My son is going through the courts requesting full custody of his daughter. It has been very emotional for us, and I am having a hard time stopping the tears. My granddaughter's mother—they did not marry—just moved her five states away. Please assist in a loving way to phrase the prayer."

——⋙·0·⋘——

Yes, benevolent prayers are what you say for other people, whereas MBO requests are strictly for specific things for you. A whole different set of angels takes care of those requests. Perhaps you could say:

> *Benevolent Prayer*
>
> *"I ask that any and all beings assist my granddaughter in having the most benevolent living arrangement and custody situation for her, thank you!"*

Remember that all these requests have to be benevolent for everyone in the request, and saying a benevolent prayer puts it squarely on what's best for the child—whether that's full custody, partial custody or whatever. Remember that there are soul contracts at work here, so you can only request what's best for the child and her soul contract. When the court case comes up you can say:

Benevolent Prayer

"I ask that any and all beings assist the judge in making the best decision for the custody of my granddaughter, thank you!"

FAMILY REUNIONS AND TRIPS

Kelly has a number of MBO stories to relate, which I have condensed a little.

Kelly writes: "I have a number of MBOs to share with you, all of which happened this past weekend. My family and I were to attend a family reunion in Iowa, and upon arrival to our first hotel, I requested an MBO that my husband would be able to upgrade our reservation to a suite at no extra cost. The chances seemed slim as there was a convention going on and the hotel was busy. We were given a suite, however!

"I then requested an MBO the next day so that our next hotel room would be affordable in such a way that money would unexpectedly come to us to cover the extra costs of a larger suite than we usually reserved easily and effortlessly. It was at a hotel we usually stayed at for this annual gathering, but we decided upon a larger room. It just so happens that other members of my family of origin were staying there too, and upon our arrival, we were told our room was paid for—my father picked up the tab. Generally, payments were completed the following morning and my father usually arrived at the hotel after us on the first day. This was a bit unusual for us this year, as he had beaten us there and paid for the room in advance.

"I then requested an MBO to strike up harmonious conversations where I would make some solid heartfelt connections. This, I usually felt was quite unlikely, as in the past, I've been the black sheep and odd one of my family, the one people strived to understand but just couldn't. Well, over the years I'd kept to myself a lot. This year, one aunt and one cousin really connected with me. I found out we had much more in common than any of us had thought. It was so relieving for me as these gatherings had, in the past, tended to be tense for me. Children also seemed to gravitate to me and sit with me and this brought other people. I didn't have to go far, as people came to me. I felt more accepted than I had in prior years.

"I also requested an MBO en route to my home to find some hibiscus tea. I had not had luck thus far, and when I arrived at the town in which I'd requested to find it, I found it in the second shop I entered—only one variety and only three boxes available. Perfect!

"I became more open about my MBO requests and stated them aloud with my immediate family present. By this time, my youngest son was convinced this really worked. My older one was beginning to see some real synchronicity and was asking pertinent questions that you answer in your first book: 'Why do we have to say it aloud or write it?' And my husband was beginning to really listen. I was having a ball, because they kept coming true, and it got to a point where I'd say it and just expect the result. They always worked! I asked for a swift and safe trip home with smooth-flowing traffic. This was right after my husband mentioned that he knew we'd hit the 'returning home from the weekend away' traffic. He chuckled when I said 'And may it be even better than I can hope or expect.' You never know. There wasn't any traffic stopping us the whole way home!

"Also, as we traveled, I crocheted. At one point, I realized I couldn't find my pattern. I needed it to complete my afghan, which was nearly finished. Only one thing to do when my search failed—request an MBO. So I did. Immediately after saying it, my husband reached down onto the floor between us and picked up my pattern. He had not noticed it before. My youngest son was clearly enthralled by this and how immediately it had happened. So was I!"

For Houseplants

Also from Kelly: "I requested an MBO so that my plants would receive enough water from the rain and not be parched while we were gone. The forecast didn't look like rain was in the picture. When we returned home, I didn't have to rush to water them. It was obvious it had rained, as the pavement was wet. Also, I requested, along with my son, that our pet rabbit would be taken care of—even in a spiritual sense—so he wouldn't feel he was lacking food. This was the second time we had left him for a two- to three-day time frame. He did okay last time, but he had been getting used to more regular feedings throughout the day and not all given at once. My son and I asked that any and all beings would come to his aid and comfort, a benevolent prayer, so that he would manage comfortably until we returned. He still had some food left. We also imagined pictures in our minds and sent them to him, that we wouldn't be long and that he was loved. I think the thoughts made it to him.

"My whole family is becoming a group of believers. Personally, I feel I don't believe it works—I know it does!"

CHAPTER SIX

BENEVOLENT OUTCOMES FOR HEALTH

H ere are some great stories I received from people with minor to serious medical problems. Just remember that nothing is impossible with a little assistance from your own guardian angel!

Rick wrote: "Here's one for you, Tom. I went for an eye exam today. I had all the preliminary work done by office technicians, then waited approximately fifteen minutes for the doctor. I stood in the doorway so I could at least watch television from my exam room. I turned, went back into my exam room and quietly asked, 'I request a most benevolent outcome for the doctor to see me immediately.' I walked to the doorway, and there he was, right on cue!"

⟶⊙⟵

I've actually done this so many times that I forget to mention it. It can really speed things up. I'll also say this on my way to an appointment, whether it's a doctor, dentist or whomever:

Most Benevolent Outcome

*"I request a most benevolent outcome that the
doctor will see me promptly and that my visit will
be benevolent for me, thank you!"*

So what to do if you're running late? As I mentioned in the first book, I simply say:

Most Benevolent Outcome

*"I request a compression of time until
(whatever hour you wish to choose), thank you!"*

We are able to manipulate time somewhat these days. After you say this, do not look at your watch or the clock in your car. Simply drive to your destination and you'll be amazed that you arrive right on time, or even a couple of minutes early. This also works if you have a lot of work to get done and are running behind. Experiment with this, as it's a valuable tool. I use it all the time.

GENTLE DOCTOR VISITS

Nancy writes: "I have started requesting MBOs daily, and they make my day run smoothly. I am a seventy-year-old retiree, so having days run well without any glitches is so helpful. Doctor's visits run on time and are easily accomplished without any distressing news; problems seem to resolve themselves fairly easily. Thanks a lot. I really appreciate your work."

———

As I have mentioned many times in my previous articles, for those of you who have not yet made requesting benevolent outcomes a habit, this makes your daily life easier and gentler. It lowers stress, the fear factor and probably your blood pressure—just in time!

DENTAL DISCOUNT

Pam writes on Facebook: "Hi Tom, I just wanted to share a great MBO I had today; thank you for telling me all about MBOs. I'm having some dental work done soon and the cost was a lot. I did an MBO for the cost to be a lot lower than the quote. Then the dentist office called and gave me a $1,000 discount for paying up front in full. Now, how great is that? Thank you so much."

MAMMOGRAM BENEVOLENT OUTCOME

Thelma writes: "Greetings. I must tell you that I am so grateful that I was introduced to your book. I have not veered from using MBOs daily. I must share this great experience with you.

"I was requested to do some routine medical tests, and to be candid, even though I know I needed to do them, I was still nervous. Well, I did do them after requesting an MBO, and most of the tests came back clear—with the exception of a small cyst in my kidney, which is not a threat. I had to do a mammogram also, which I had not done since 1999 (shame on me, but I was not ready for any disturbing news). The report came back reporting calcifications in both breasts. This I had known before and had me concerned. The lab then requested that I return, as they did not have any record of my past visit in 1999. My daughter, who is very meticulous and is also a doctor herself, was able to produce the written report from 1999 and demanded that they find the x-ray films. At this time, I was due for a more in-depth mammogram for comparison. This had me more shaken, although I had my daughter's full support.

"I must joyfully report that I repeated my MBOs for them to find their records and not find any change in nine years while on my way to repeat the mammogram yesterday. I got to the lab, with the staff fully alerted by my daughter. I dressed down and was ready to go when a technician came out and apologized for my having to return and told me I could get dressed and go as they had found the records. The doctors went over them and there had been no change since 1999. I will be forever grateful to you for sharing MBOs."

WEIGHT LOSS

Karin in Canada asked about what benevolent outcomes to request to lose weight. I think there are various MBOs to request. You can request an MBO for the perfect weight for you, you can request MBOs to find the best diet plan for your body or you can request an MBO to be filled without gorging. I'm sure there are others that you will think of, such as requesting MBOs to eat reasonably when you go out for dinner and to choose the right foods in the grocery store. The angels are always there!

Helena emailed asking what benevolent prayer she could say for her sister who has a weight problem brought on from early life experiences. I suggested she say:

Benevolent Prayer

> "I ask that any and all beings assist and aid my sister
> in being led to understand her eating disorder and that
> she be led to successful treatments that will be most
> benevolent for her, thank you!"

Helena writes: "I have been meaning to send you a thank you for kindly replying to my questions about my sister's weight issues that I had been worried about. I have been saying the benevolent prayer for her that you suggested. My sister went to the hospital to have her blood pressure taken and that was fine, but now she is being sent to someone to help her with her weight. How about that for a benevolent answer? She has never been helped like that before! I told her that I had been saying benevolent prayers for her, and she could not believe it. Now I hope I have the same luck, as I am still requesting an MBO for finding a job for me. But what fabulous help for my sister. I have also gotten my nieces hooked on your book; they have just bought a copy."

MORE WEIGHT LOSS

Frances writes: "I have struggled with being overweight all of my life. I ask for MBOs to help me with this, yet I feel that nothing much has happened, or nothing much that I can perceive. Could you help with a suggested MBO for healthy weight loss and good eating habits? Thanks."

For Frances and anyone else with this challenge, I'll give you some MBOs to request and then some practical suggestions. You can say, "I request a most benevolent outcome for attaining the best weight for my health and happiness, thank you! I request a most benevolent outcome for choosing the healthiest foods both at home and in restaurants, thank you! I request a most benevolent outcome for being led to healthy, enjoyable exercises for me, thank you!"

Now, having had a weight problem myself in the past, and still having to continually watch myself (thanks to my wife), we both found that Weight Watchers® worked the best of any program we ever tried. I lost twenty-five pounds.

The best thing that came out of the program was portion control. Most restaurants serve twice what you should consume. Therefore, my wife and I either split the entree or divide it into two halves and take the other half and have it the next day or two days. During our Sedona trip, for a week we did just that almost every dinner, lunches too, and did not have our first desert until Tuesday evening (we arrived Friday morning) when we split a mousse.

The Weight Watchers® Smart Ones® and Lean Cuisine® both list the Weight Watchers points, although we don't count anymore. It's best to not eat out of the container, but spread it out on a plate. They normally take up the whole plate, so visually you feel like you're eating a full meal.

As for exercise, start walking if you are not already. Either early in the morning or evening get out and walk for at least twenty minutes. It really does boost your metabolism. I hope I've been of some assistance!

FOR RELEASING BACK PAIN

Linda writes: "I had the most wonderful results from an MBO this morning. The past couple of days I have had such pain in my back. It started when I woke up Wednesday morning and nothing I did made it go away. I tried hot baths, which usually help, but not this time. I also work part time in addition to my full-time job and last night on the way home I was just so tired and my back hurt so badly that I was talking to my angels on the way home telling them how bad I felt and how tired I was. I then did an MBO for getting some much-needed sleep and to wake up pain-free in the morning.

"When I got home I didn't even go to bed but lay down on the loveseat in my living room. I should probably mention that I'd worked from 7:00 PM until 4:00 AM and had gotten home around 4:30 AM. When I woke up this morning, the first thing I noticed when I sat up was that the pain from my back was all gone. I said a very heartfelt thank you to my angels. What a relief! I do love MBOs, and I can't wait for your new book to come out. I keep *The Gentle Way* right in my living room and read out of it every couple of days. Thank you so much for writing your book and thanks to your guardian angel for his help too!"

AT THE EYE DOCTOR AND AT THE ORTHODONTIST

Also from Linda: Last Friday I asked for an MBO for Ben's eye doctor appointment. He's been wearing glasses for two years for reading and last year he lost them. Getting new ones was something else I'd been putting off. I also was told he had astigmatism. We went to the appointment and found out he has 20/20 vision—without glasses! There was no evidence of astigmatism, either. I asked how that was possible. The doctor was new, and he said, 'I don't know, but I checked him two different ways.' Then he joked and said, 'I healed him just by having him come to the office,' and he laughed. I laughed too. If he only knew! Thank you and your angels so much for bringing this to us."

Kelly writes: "I want to share another benevolent outcome situation with you. The other day, my son came home from school with his retainer broken. He had somehow broken off a small wire spring. Upon looking at it, it seemed as though it would have to be replaced altogether, but I wasn't about to give up hope. I scheduled an orthodontic appointment for him and while we were en route, I requested aloud an MBO for the appointment to result in no costs to us, so that there would be no charge for whatever had to be done for my son's retainer situation.

"Sure enough, the orthodontist stated that at first he was a bit worried due to the nature of the break in the appliance, but he somehow managed to bend the remaining spring just so and it met my son's needs perfectly. He told me to be sure to tell the receptionist that this visit was to be no charge to us. Apparently, retainer repairs can generally incur additional costs. This was all new to us, and we are so grateful for this outcome!

RECOVERING FROM ADDICTION

Jill writes: "My sister sent me the link for your site. I say my requests for MBOs daily and realize they have given me great strength. I seem to have a lot going on around me and am often unable to see the forest for the trees—crisis in my marriage, sexual addiction, my own alcohol and food addictions, unclear direction, unemployment and no income. I am also facing an international move in three months with no direction as to where we go.

"I say the same MBOs daily. Should I change them each day? I am not sure what to ask for with so much going on. At best I ask for strength and feel I am receiving that. Keep up the good work and thank you very much!"

―――――⇒⋅⊙⋅⇐―――――

May I suggest for Jill, and for anyone else with any of these challenges, you say:

> *Most Benevolent Outcome*
> "I request a most benevolent outcome for being led to the best treatments for me for overcoming my addictions, thank you!"

Don't forget that you can request an MBO for the perfect job for you and for the perfect place to live.

RECOVERING FROM CANCER

Vicki in Texas writes: "This week we were back at the hospital in Houston for the second time this month. My husband has new cancer in the lymph nodes behind his sternum. He has been battling thyroid cancer since 2004. I requested an MBO of strength and resilience for both of us. We have been amazed how we are not in a state of fear or worry, and I know it is due to the MBOs. If you have any suggestions as to how to improve our use of MBOs in matters of health and healing, we would love to hear from you. Thank you for introducing us to MBOs and for the affect they have had on our lives."

―――――§―0―《―――――

For Vicki and anyone else with family health problems right now, you can say a benevolent prayer such as:

《《《《《《《《《《《《《《《《《《《《《《《《《《《 *Benevolent Prayer* 《《《《《《《《《《《《《《《《《《《《《《《《《《
> *"I ask that any and all beings assist my husband in being led to treatments that will be the most beneficial and most benevolent for him, thank you!"*

Notice how they have no fear? I've reported on this in the past when I had to undergo surgery for congestive heart failure. And if the health problem is yours, you can request an MBO by saying:

《《 《《 《《 《《 《《 《《 《《 《《 *Most Benevolent Outcome* 《《 《《 《《 《《 《《 《《 《《 《《
> *"I request a most benevolent outcome for this treatment (surgery, and so on), and may I be led to the most beneficial treatments for me, thank you!"*

As a side note: I don't know why we've had so many people named Diane writing in. Perhaps it's numerological in nature— but they are all different people.

Diane writes: "I wrote to you in the fall about MBOs regarding breast cancer. I had had a follow-up mammogram at a specialized breast care center and further results from an MRI, which indicated that a biopsy was needed. I kept requesting MBOs and with one thing and another, I couldn't get an appointment to see the MD until March. I wanted to discuss the MRI results before deciding upon the biopsy.

"When I arrived, the nurse asked me to change into a gown. I said I wasn't there for a procedure, but was there to talk to the MD. She went to check, and when she returned she offered me three options: 1) it was time for a six-month follow-up mammogram, which I could do and then see the MD; 2) I could return in three months and get a second MRI; or 3) I could talk to the MD. I chose option one. The breast care specialist shared with me the radiologist's report that I had no changes from the last mammogram. I had no cancer. She sent a report to my internist saying that they'd used a computer to verify the mammogram results and that I had no cancer. It was not necessary to have a biopsy. I was very, very grateful. Thank you very much for sharing MBOs."

For Seizures

Marcy writes: "I noticed someone write in recently asking what to say for an MBO for cancer. I have a twenty-eight-year-old son who has seizures. Would you please give us the words to say for an MBO for seizures?"

For him, he should say:

Most Benevolent Outcome
"I request an MBO that my seizures be mild and that over time they occur less and less, thank you!"

Naturally, he could change that up to fit his circumstances more accurately. For you, say a benevolent prayer:

Benevolent Prayer

"I ask that any and all beings assist my son in reducing the severity of his seizures, thank you!"

And you can say an MBO for yourself:

Most Benevolent Outcome

"I request an MBO for being led to treatments for my son that will be the most benevolent for him, and may they be even better than I can hope for or expect, thank you!"

AT THE DOCTOR'S OFFICE AGAIN

I condensed the following story a little, but I didn't wish to truncate the message, as I think you'll find it interesting.

Kelly writes: "I have an MBO to share with you—actually, a double one. I had two medical appointments scheduled for Friday the fourth— 4/4. (Being intrigued by numerology, I chose that date purposely, as my life path number is 4.) Anyway, I felt I wanted more assurance that I would receive positive outcomes from both appointments, so I asked for most benevolent outcomes for both. The first one was a follow-up mammogram, as I had undergone a stereotactic biopsy six months prior where the results were negative, merely calcifications. I asked that the test go smoothly and come out with normal, healthy results. It did! Now I have another six months until my annual screening mammogram. I'll be sure to ask for an MBO again.

"The second appointment involved a visit to a new MD, specifically a liver specialist. I asked for the most benevolent outcome for the visit to the new specialist: that I would feel comfortable with this new doctor, that I would be regarded as very healthy and that there would be no concerns regarding the issue at hand. Well, I immediately knew I liked the place. A little glitch happened in that my primary MD hadn't sent my records as planned, but the appointment continued with this new MD taking my history and going through my understanding of the situation/concerns.

"The doctor was one of the most thorough I'd ever met or worked with, and there was an immediate rapport. He specifically liked the fact that I work for the same hospital he does, only I'm a speech-language pathologist. He did find one thing that was curious—my hands are orangey. I'd noticed that myself a month or so prior. His first question was if I ate a lot of carrots. Sure enough, I ate those, as well as mangoes, squash, sweet potatoes, papaya and numerous other high vitamin A-rich foods, not to mention the fact my multivitamin contains Vitamin A. In fact, I'd noticed over the course of the prior several months that I had been craving orange foods. I interpreted this as being because I was addressing second chakra issues in some way. This MD termed my condition possibly carotenemia, which results from excess vitamin A consumption. Well, I was relieved that he felt there was likely no real concern, but he needed to see the blood work and we'd speak over the phone once he did. Although when I left his office I didn't yet know all that was to come, I felt at peace and certain that there was really no concern.

"The following Monday, the doctor called me after having received my blood work results and said that the minor elevations really didn't concern him and that he didn't feel it necessary to do anything—just a follow-up in six months. So I received another MBO with this appointment. I'll be requesting one for the next appointment in six months' time. I want to add, when this doctor took my pulse, he held both of my wrists simultaneously, with each of his hands wrapped around my wrists securely. As he did this, I felt electricity go straight down my fingers to my fingertips—very faint, but noticeable. I felt charged. Maybe the angels are working through him in some way; whatever the case, it was a most benevolent day for me.

"I'd like to mention also that when I made the second appointment about three weeks in advance, I was told that the only day he had any openings available in April was on the fourth. So I also feel the vibrations of that day were good in general, but the likelihood of there being an opening on my target date intrigues me. I hadn't asked for an MBO when scheduling. I do need to remember to ask more habitually. As it stands now, I tend to remember when I'm driving. I've been getting loads of great parking spaces!

"Thank you so much for allowing me to share my stories and thank you also for making the public aware of this valuable assistance from our divine companions."

CHAPTER SEVEN

BENEVOLENT OUTCOMES AT THE HOSPITAL

I was driving to Fort Worth, Texas, to speak and do a book signing. It was raining, and it seemed that I picked up a respiratory cough that over the next few days, would not go away. As I was scheduled to be in Houston on September 17 for a talk at a church, I wanted to make sure it did not develop into something more severe, so I visited my pulmonary doctor, thinking that he would give me an inhaler to solve the problem.

Instead, he informed me that my lungs were full of liquid because I was experiencing congestive heart failure. My heart was beating at over 130 beats per minute. He said I was going straight to the hospital, located in an adjacent building. I told him, "I'm glad I wore my clean undies today!" Naturally, I immediately requested a most benevolent outcome as I walked over to the admissions office. After they checked me in and assigned me to a room, I went up to the floor, checked in with the nurses' station and settled in. I called my wife and told her that she would never guess where I was. They did all the normal tests—EKG, x-rays, blood work—and started me on some medicine through the IV they had installed.

The next morning they took me down to the surgery room where I was scheduled to have a tube run through an artery from my groin up to my heart to check for blood clots, and then they were going to shock my heart to see if it would return to a normal rhythm. In congestive heart failure, the top chambers of the heart flutter or fibrillate and do not supply sufficient blood to the lower chambers. Of course I said:

Most Benevolent Outcome

"I request a most benevolent outcome for both procedures today. Thank you!"

I can relate now that I had absolutely no fear. I joked with the doctor, nurses and three student nurses, and they asked if I would allow them to watch the procedure. I said sure—they needed to learn somehow, so why not with me? I also said a benevolent prayer that any and all beings would assist the doctors and nurses in the procedure.

I awoke from the anesthesia to hear that they had shocked my heart three times, but it still would not return to a normal rhythm. I found this a little strange, as I had requested a benevolent outcome for the procedure. I know, after requesting these around 15,000 times over the years, that they work perfectly—just sometimes not in the way we think they should work. So I had faith that whatever lay before me was going to be the most benevolent outcome for me.

Back in my room, the doctor came and explained that since the procedure had not worked, they were putting me on a different medicine and scheduling me for another type of procedure. I spent the weekend watching college football, and then on Sunday professional football. The hospital I was in had only a limited number of cable channels, so it was a real chore to find something to watch to pass the time. Visits from my family and friends were greatly appreciated.

On Tuesday, September 12, they wheeled me down again to a staging area. This time they had a cardiac surgeon who specialized in electrical work, as he called it. There are only three doctors who do this procedure in Dallas, and he was known as the best, performing fifteen to twenty of these procedures a week. I thought that getting the best guy in the business in Dallas was a benevolent outcome. Again, before wheeling me into the surgical room, I was joking with the anesthesiologist and nurses. I sang a song with one of them and kidded one who forgot to pick up food for one of the staff members. I had no fear or stress after requesting a benevolent outcome.

The procedure the doctor performed was to run three or four catheters up a vein from my groin into the top chambers of my heart, where he located the misfiring cells and destroyed them. My heart immediately went back into a normal rhythm—a most benevolent outcome!

I was released the next day and started my recovery. I was even able to travel to Houston for my scheduled talk and book signing. Because of my stay in the hospital, I had to cancel my trip to the Frankfurt Book Fair, where I'd planned to sell the foreign rights to my book. So naturally I wanted to know why this had occurred when it did, preventing me from expanding the number of my readers. I was given a couple of answers on this.

First I was told that I would be much too busy and someone else would be selling those rights. The second reason was a real eye opener. It was explained to me that my soul was quite happy, as I had been able to rid myself of a karmic debt that was at least 200 years old. It seems that in a war, I killed some people, but even though it was war, I had brought grief and heartache to their families, so now I needed to literally experience heartache and a broken heart.

I pondered this for a few days, and then I asked about saying a benevolent prayer for those families. I was told that I could say a prayer for these families and that it would have long-term benefits for me. So here is the benevolent prayer that I said:

Benevolent Prayer

"I ask that any and all beings come to the aid and comfort of the families of the people that I have slain in a past life."

But as I said this prayer each morning over the next several days, it did not seem sufficient. I felt it was lacking something. So then I was inspired—those whispers in my ear—to add this:

Benevolent Prayer

"I ask that any and all beings come to the aid and comfort of all those I have harmed either physically, emotionally, mentally or spiritually in any past, present or future life and that any and all beings come to the aid and comfort of the families of those I have harmed in any way in any past, present or future life, thank you."

So I began saying this prayer almost every day in the morning when I said my daily affirmation. But then I began to wonder if I was saying the prayer too many times for it to be effective and asked about it in my meditation. This is the answer I received from Theo:

No. You should continue, as you notice that you do get a warm feeling from doing so, although you do not always notice it. It is a feeling of love that is sent to you by those angels that handle your request, and it will bring aid and comfort to all those people on a daily basis, or as many times as you remember to say the prayer. It is something that, as I said, has long-term benefits beyond what you might think or consider. It is a way of wiping out many karmic debts, because you are saying a prayer for all those people and it is highly unusual for anyone to think of doing that in a present life.

❋   ❋   ❋

I made another change in the original prayer thanks to a reader who suggested that I add the words "and friends" right after the original word "families." So here is the complete daily benevolent prayer I say each day:

Benevolent Prayer

"I ask that any and all beings come to the aid and comfort of anyone I have ever harmed either physically, mentally, emotionally, morally or spiritually in any past, present or future life and that any and all beings come to the aid and comfort of the families and friends of those I have ever harmed in any way in any past, present or future life, thank you."

This is the greatest gift you can ever give yourself for all your upcoming and past lives. It may be hard to believe, but Theo has assured me over and over that this works.

In February of 2008, I was down to two medicines and taking them in much smaller amounts, but I was having short-term memory loss. My electro-cardiologist said one of my medicines was having a neurological side effect and gave me two options. Door number one was two nights in the hospital while they monitored me for a new medicine. Door number two was one night in the hospital with another procedure to go into both ventricles, with only an 80 percent success rate. Going on another medicine—especially one that might have other side effects—wasn't very appealing, so I chose option number two.

Naturally, I requested MBOs for the procedure and said benevolent prayers for the surgeon and the whole staff. The procedure was a success and allowed me to get rid of those last two medicines. Now the only excuse I have for not remembering something is a "senior moment."

Breast Cancer

On March 13, 2008, my wife had breast cancer surgery. When Dena discovered a small lump just under the skin, she decided to have a plastic surgeon remove it to have the least amount of scarring possible. Naturally, we requested benevolent outcomes for the procedure and I said a benevolent prayer.

When we got the biopsy back that it was an invasive cancer, he referred her to two doctors—one at Presbyterian and a doctor at Baylor Medical here in Dallas. We first visited the doctor at Presbyterian and he was horrible—one horror story after another instead of saying "this is what we do first," and so on—he had no information yet from the first surgeon, and he even used his pen to mark on her breast. We left wondering how could this guy treat women like that.

Next was the Baylor doctor, and she was much better (we were requesting MBOs for her to be okay). The plastic surgeon had said "margins" would be needed, and he said it should only be at most three times the black-eyed-pea-sized lump he'd removed. She insisted on this with the cancer doctor.

Dena decided to delay the operation in order to get on alternative therapies—vitamins, special drinks and listening to healing CDs by Dick Sutphen. I suggested March 13, as that is astrologically trine her July 13 birth date. As I mentioned above (with requests for a benevolent outcome and a benevolent prayer), she had the surgery and the doctor limited her "margins" to a slightly wider area, against her advice to us.

She had an appointment this week to receive the results of the biopsy. They showed no cancer at all! Thanks to everyone who said a benevolent prayer for her. I will also say that even with this news, the doctor tried to talk her into having radiation or chemotherapy, which she refused. She feels that with her lifestyle change and all the vitamins she now takes, the odds are greatly reduced of the cancer reappearing. So the lesson here is, don't always accept what a doctor tells you. They are in their own box of beliefs and what they accept as usual procedures. Listen to those whispers in your ear for guidance and request MBOs to be led to the best treatments for you!

HOSPITAL BILLS

A lady who asked me to change her name to **Joy writes:** "In December I emailed you about a huge hospital bill for which I wanted to have a benevolent outcome. You gave me the wording:

Most Benevolent Outcome

"I request a most benevolent outcome for being able to pay my hospital expenses, and may the results be better than I hope for or expect, thank you!"

"Well, today I called the hospital's patient financial services as I had gotten a notice that I was in collections about the bills. Come to find out that the letters crossed in the mail—so now, instead of owing over $52,000, they knocked the bill down to a little over $2,000!"

———≫-0-≪———

When I'm speaking before a group, I normally use the metaphor of being on a dusty, rocky road with a mass of other people, but just on the side of the road is this gentle path— the gentle way. When you take that path, it doesn't mean that you're going to have a boring life. There are still those major "speed bumps" on the path, but you cross them much more easily than if you had been on that rocky, dusty road.

THE ASPIRIN ANGEL

Debrah writes: "I have found that there is an angel energy for any and all requests. Like if I am more tired and achy than usual, I ask for a healing, like aspirin, from a being who I call the aspirin angel. It's the same in any and all requests of a benevolent nature and for the greatest good of all concerned. If I need to feel the presence of their love, I ask for and am open to receive that love. If I am tired and I am placed into a position of serving many people, I ask for the strength to be my best and they always comply. One must be open to receiving. I see myself as a large satellite dish, open to cosmic higher vibrations, and yes, I have worked on my stuff with higher guidance for a while. I trust the process totally. Maybe you could cover this, this having no fear and trusting the process, for the universe only says yes. Try it yourself—the aspirin angel, that is. You will love it."

——————•-0-•——————

This reminds me of a book (I can't recall the title) that talks about asking for various angels to assist you in your daily life. Accounting angels, driving angels and work angels were mentioned. I thought the book was a basic book that would get everyone thinking about angelic assistance, but the problem I foresaw is that you had to think up a different angel for each duty. In reality, all these angels are just your guardian angel and guides—at least that's what I'm told. I know it surely makes things easier only having to talk to my own guardian angel. But I did want to ask Theo so that I could give Debrah more information.

Theo, how does a request for an "aspirin angel" really work?

A good question, Tom. As you might guess, energy is sent from their guardian angel that contains much love and gentle feelings so that the person is wrapped in this energy field and they receive warm feelings that are a natural pick-me-up. We are here to answer those requests, but again, you have to ask before we can send this energy. And we are happy to do it and will joyfully do so when a person requests this energy.

✳ ✳ ✳

I suggest that if you want this energy, you say:

> *Most Benevolent Outcome*
>
> "I request a most benevolent outcome for you to send loving, gentle healing energy to me that will be the most benevolent for me at this time, thank you!"

Diane wrote about a trip to the emergency room, and this seems to tie in with the above—synchronicity again!

Diane writes: "Last night I got home and started to feel sick. I was dizzy and started feeling hot and then cold. Then I started to throw up. Things were not getting any better, and about three hours later, I asked my husband to take me to the emergency ward of the local hospital. While I was sitting there waiting for my test results and feeling horrible, I thought of doing an MBO. Well, I did feel a lot better—not 100 percent, but at least I was able to walk and felt that my stomach had settled. I took medication this morning and have started an MBO to get me through the day at work. So far so good!"

STRESS AT THE SURGICAL CLINIC

Helena previously wrote me when she was out of work asking for an MBO. Now she has found work as a receptionist in a surgical clinic, but she's stressed, as the doctors and nurses are not nice to her or the other receptionists. I'm condensing her email, as it was long and detailed.

Helena asked: "I was wondering if you could help me with the right wording for requesting MBOs for 1) getting on and fitting in with the doctors and the other receptionists 2) protecting me from the doctors and other receptionists, and 3) being able to do and understand everything that I am expected to do and understand.

"I am worried about being able to stick the job out, and I want to enjoy it but I never realized how hard and stressful it is. I know that two of the receptionists will be leaving soon because they have had enough of the way they are being treated. Although we all work so hard, there is hardly any fun and laughter in the place.

"I am a healer, and although I have told some of the receptionists, they think I am odd for being into healing. I am not ashamed of this, and they do make me laugh with their responses. I just want to be able to fit in with everyone and do everything that is expected of me as a receptionist. So far I am a nervous wreck because I am under so much pressure, and I don't feel that the receptionists and doctors are nice or helpful toward me. I am too frightened to speak out in case I lose my job."

These suggestions are not only for Helena but also for anyone else who finds herself in a similar situation. Perhaps you were put there to be the candle in the dark. You're in a room of stress as medical personnel try their best—they are under extremely trying circumstances themselves. So what can you do to lighten up the place? I'm going to give you some suggestions, but I don't know if you can implement all of them. Do the ones you can.

Each day when you go to work say:

Most Benevolent Outcome

"I request a most benevolent outcome for my workday.
May my work be productive and without error, and
may the results of this workday be even better than
I can hope for or expect, thank you!"

Print this out in big letters and say it before you go out the door each day. This sets it up for your guardian angel to do some amazing things with your day.

Are you allowed to place a sign on the wall in front of your workstation? If so, why not put up the Expect Great Things sign that you can print out from my website? Naturally, you can say this each time you come to work, but it will also be there available for others to read—and you want them to.

Each day you can say a benevolent prayer for everyone you work with. Say:

Benevolent Prayer

"I ask that any and all beings send loving and calming energy to all the doctors and other medical personnel in this facility and surround them with loving pink light all day, thank you!"

Is there a place where you could put up funny cartoons about doctors and nurses that would make others laugh? Laughter is great for the soul. You can find them online by doing a Google search. Then cut them out and put them on a bulletin board, above your desk or in the lunchroom. If anyone sees you doing it, just say you think the place needs a little laughter and humor. Perhaps others will start to do the same thing.

Remember, healer—you can be the healer of healers. Be that beautiful light.

Helena recently wrote back with the following news: "I wanted to email you to tell you what happened to me. I previously emailed you to tell you about my stressful job working as a receptionist in a surgery clinic, and I asked if you could help me with some MBOs for help in my job.

"Last week, after reading an article about a man who can tell you things about yourself through a tea leaf reading, I decided to ring him for a consultation. Halfway through my reading he asked me why he could see a lot of pink light around me. He kept going on about me being showered with beautiful pink light. This made me gasp and giggle. Isn't that proof that my requesting an MBO to be surrounded with pink light is definitely working for me? I had never met the tea leaf reading man before. How brilliant is that?"

BLOOD CLOTS

Mary Ann writes: "In February I developed blood clots, one of which passed through the right side of my heart. The heart passed the clots to the lungs, and I had multiple clots in both lungs. I was in the intensive care unit for nine days. Other complications developed and it was discovered that I was swollen with fluid that had ovarian cancer cells in it. Three and a half years ago, I recovered from ovarian cancer, and I was very upset to hear it was back, especially since I had the complication of blood clots.

"I began to ask for an MBO to reduce the excess fluid in my swollen legs, feet and belly, asking that it be expelled from my body. In a very short time I began to expel the fluid. My feet and legs and belly are almost completely normal now. I have to get chemotherapy every week, but I am getting stronger every day and am very pleased with my progress. As you can tell, I have plenty more to request along my road to recovery, but I want to thank you and tell everyone that this is very successful."

PARALYSIS

Annette writes: "I have been hoping to get my Reiki practice started. In addition to a regular practice, I want to volunteer with patients who are veterans, especially those with post-traumatic

stress syndrome and head trauma and also with cancer patients.
I want to offer Reiki to help facilitate their healing, as well as
working with police, firefighters and other rescuers to help
reduce their stress. I was put in touch with a woman who was
looking for an acupuncturist to help her daughter who had been
seriously injured in a car accident—major head trauma. The person mentioned to her that I was a Reiki Master, and after a few
days, she requested my services. Normally I would not charge
to do Reiki in this case, but I had to travel (an hour's drive) so
I requested mileage and then said that if she wanted to make a
donation, fine, and if not, then that was fine as well. We agreed
on an amount and on Memorial Day, I traveled to the nursing
home where she was. I asked for an MBO for good weather
and safe travel with little traffic. The rain and storms we were
suppose to have all day let up just in time for me to leave, and
the traffic on the interstate was minimal—unusual for a holiday,
especially with the state parks and lakes nearby! By the time the
session was done, the weather had cleared up and the sun came
out in time for the patient to be taken outside and for me to
have a nice evening drive home. Thank you, my guardian angel!
Then, when I looked in the envelope, not only did she pay me
the mileage, but another $50 extra!

"Now for the most interesting MBO. This was so amazing
that I wanted to share it with you. I asked for an MBO for the
Reiki session with the client with the head trauma. I felt that
she had brain damage but was 'in' there. As I worked and gave
Reiki, I got responses from her. The doctors said she was not
responding, and they were planning on moving her to a nursing
facility and away from the brain injury rehabilitation center.

"I knew she was communicating, and I knew she communicated with me. She was paralyzed on her right side and had

movement of her left hand, but she was not able to control it as well as she would like. I felt so much from her when I did the initial scan and felt it was vital that she be able to give the doctors the sign they needed to continue her rehab. I felt that she would never be 'the same,' but that she had a chance to recover some of her abilities and was fighting and trying hard to come back. There were noticeable signs of improvement the next day when she moved he lips in a pucker to kiss her Mom and was able to control her arm enough to hug her, something she had not been able to do before my treatment."

Later, Annette sent another email to update me: "I just got the most wonderful news! The young lady I told you about, whom I did Reiki work with in the nursing home, actually fed herself yesterday! The doctors had told her mother that she was unable to formulate thoughts or respond to stimuli and would never be able to be more than in a vegetative state. After I did the initial scan, I knew they were wrong.

"Her mother decided to try to feed her some baby food she had liked as a child, and after the first mouthful, she took the spoon from her mother and began feeding herself! This is major. Her mom ran out and the first person she saw was a custodian who came in, saw what was happening and ran down the hall to get the nurse. Several nurses came and documented the event. Everyone was amazed, and I was so grateful to all the angelic beings who helped me be the vessel for this Reiki work.

"Another bit of encouraging news—she has shown slight movement in the hand on the side that is paralyzed. I am going back in a week to facilitate healing for the surgery. With the help of my guardian angel, I will do two more healings for free."

CHAPTER EIGHT

THE TRANSITION OF JOY

M ost of my stories I write about are how great requesting benevolent outcomes are for relieving stress and reducing the fear factor in life to the point where it almost doesn't exist. One of my friends, Joy, along with her husband Robert, had been requesting benevolent outcomes for several years; I even related a couple of stories about the two of them in my first book. In January 2008, she was involved in an automobile wreck on a highway near their home that required the intervention of her guardian angel.

She was traveling at about 60 to 65 miles per hour in rainy conditions when she was suddenly struck from behind by a truck that the wrecker driver later estimated had to have been going at least 80 to 100 mph. He expressed his surprise that she hadn't rolled her car. She was knocked off the road and somehow came to a stop about a fourth of a mile down the highway, but still to this day does not remember how she did it. At the time, she didn't realize she was injured but discovered a couple of broken bones later. The driver of the truck told her he was on his cell phone at the time, and he told the police officer he'd reached down for something and taken his eyes off the road.

She later told me she was positive that her guardian angel had intervened, as she could see no way she could have brought the car safely to a stop. I decided to ask my guardian angel Theo about this, and here's what I received in my meditation (which you can do too):

Yes. She is correct in this assumption, as she was stunned by the suddenness of the accident and could not have steered the car herself due to her age and reaction time. Therefore her guardian angel assisted and took over in steering her car safely to the side of the road.

✳   ✳   ✳

Later she would discover that she had suffered injuries but was in shock at the time. A little less than a year after the accident, on the afternoon of December 5, 2008, my wife received a frantic call from our friend Robert. His wife Joy, whom we had just seen at a dinner party that past Saturday, was in the hospital and had already flatlined twice. He had called us and several other friends, but we were the only ones who were able to drop what we were doing and rush to the hospital. The other couples were in different sections of the metroplex, or were hard to reach.

When we arrived at the hospital in Dallas, we went to a waiting room just outside the Intensive Care Unit (ICU). Robert, his daughter, and her daughter, husband and brother were there. We were all told by the nurse (also named Joy, which was ironic, as our Joy was a retired nurse) that Joy was in critical condition. When they had tried to put a stint in her carotid artery, her blood pressure had dropped to zero. They had to stop and then discovered that all the blood vessels leading to her heart were 80 percent blocked, which we were told is quite rare. We were ushered into the cubicle where she was and were all allowed to whisper in her ear. When it was my turn, I said, "Joy, this is Tom. I ask that any and all beings assist and comfort you for the result that will be the most benevolent for you." After we'd said goodbye after dinner the previous Saturday night I had also said a benevolent prayer for her upcoming operation.

As we all turned to return to the room, my wife saw out of the corner of her eye that Joy's blood pressure had suddenly dropped from eighty to zero again. Some of Joy's family decided to go eat, as they had had nothing all day. A few minutes later I told my wife Dena, Robert and his daughter that I would go check on her. In the cubicle, the nurses were doing heart compressions—not a good sign. They closed the curtain so I couldn't see, so I returned to the waiting room. Ten minutes later, I went back and the other end of the curtain was open. I observed them still steadily giving heart compressions.

Upon my return to the waiting room, the doctor arrived and said that it did not appear she was going to make it. Her heart was not pumping on its own, and we had been previously told that she had only a 20 percent chance of full recovery, a 30 percent chance that if she made it, there would be damage to her brain and a 50 percent chance of dying. Robert and his daughter went to her side. Shortly after they went inside, the rest of her family returned, and I immediately told them to go inside.

They all came out except Robert and said that she'd passed between 4:15 and 4:20 PM. I was asked to return to the cubicle, as Robert could not leave. I did, and I comforted him and told him that he must tell her he released her. He did. Then I said he must remember her as she looked last Saturday night and not as she lay there. I was able to escort him from the room where nurse Joy had a body release form for him to fill out.

So what can this story I've related have to do with benevolent outcomes? How could this be a benevolent outcome? I do wish to point out again that you'll find Joy's name as a contributor to both my book and my newsletters. I had asked her to write to me with a benevolent outcome on her surgery, but I'll have to do that for her.

Had she lived, she probably would have been in a vegetative state, and I know that passionate lady would not have wanted to continue on in such a way. Although we will miss her laughter, her stories and her company, this was the most benevolent outcome for her. You must all remember that sometimes benevolent outcomes are not always what we expect or wish they could be.

The Untold Story

When I originally wrote the above narrative about the passing of our good friend Joy, what I did not mention was an incident that happened on the way from the hospital to our friends' house with her daughter, family and husband following my car. It was dark, and although I had been there the previous Saturday night, I had a hard time finding the street, as there were no streetlights. I finally pulled into a side street so that my wife could find our friend's telephone number and call him for directions.

I got out of the car and went back to Joy's daughter's truck to apologize, and to tell them what we were doing. Joy's husband Robert had continued down the street and I found out later that he had given his daughter directions to the house. When I started to get back in our car, suddenly the door slammed into my head, with the corner of the door hitting me just above my eye. I was stunned for a minute, surprised that it had popped back at me, as there was not that much wind. It may even have bled a little, as I recall. Luckily, my friend had one of those mini-icepacks in the refrigerator and I applied that for an hour or so. I wound up with a real shiner of a black eye.

Later I wondered more about that, so I decided to ask Theo. Here's what I asked on December 9, 2008:

Theo, did Joy slam the car door on me, or was that an accident that I needed to endure for some reason?

There was a push from the other side.

So was Joy shoving the car door into me for some reason, and if so why? Or was it just an accident?

Yes, Tom. That was Joy shoving the door into your head. She was cross ways with you because she didn't think that her death, at that moment in time, was a benevolent outcome. She was upset, Tom, as on a physical level she didn't think she was leaving. She had blocked off that possibility–as many people do, especially if they are going to experience a sudden death of any kind. She understands much more now that it was her time to go according to her soul contract and feels sorry and regretful that she injured you.

But it must have been my soul contract to experience that, wasn't it?

In a way. What you have learned from this experience is how a person, or even their soul fragment, can act not only just after death but for months or even years afterward. That is part of the death angel's duty: to comfort them and bring them up to the next level, as they are often confused and upset.

I would like to return to the subject of soul fragments being able to move things. How is that accomplished?

Fairly easily, Tom. You just concentrate your energy in one spot—in this case, on the door of your car—and then it moves. Not so sophisticated! But yes, it is a little easier if you have just departed your body and are still focused on the earth instead of going to the next level with the death angel, whom I might mention was appalled by the violence done to you. They are much more use to simply confused and angry people, but not to the extent of souls taking physical action.

❋   ❋   ❋

Theo told me to prepare questions, that Joy would be ready to speak. I would like to communicate with the fragment of the soul we knew of as Joy.

I'm here, Tom.

I'm happy we can speak today.

I'm pleased and happy too.

So are you rested now?

Yes, quite so. I'm ready to begin anew, although I have a few more duties associated with my past life before I can move to the next one, you see.

How long does it seem you've been resting, since time is not in operation or effect there?

Quite a long time. You're correct about there being no time. I was in a very restful place.

In what sort of place have you been resting, according to your beliefs?

It was, as you might guess, a very beautiful facility with lakes and streams all around. That's what I created for myself.

Your daughter thought that your soul might have passed over the first time you flatlined. Did it happen then or some other time? When was the silver cord released?

No, it did not happen then, Tom. I was fighting and observed from above what was happening and the actions of the nurses and doctors—what some people call a near-death experience.

When did the soul that we call the death angel arrive?

She—that was the appearance she gave me—was there from the first time I flatlined until the end.

Which was when they gave up on the chest compressions?

Yes, around that time, or perhaps a little before, but certainly just about that time.

So the death angel was telling you it was time to go, yes?

Absolutely, Tom, and I was saying that it was not. I resisted leaving. The angel explained to me that my soul had chosen this time to leave. She had lots of energy, as you and Dena noticed. I saw you put your hands up with the palms facing the bed.

Did you leave then, or did you stay with Robert for a while?

I was resisting leaving the love for him that I had. I wondered how he would take care of himself, but I was assured by the death angel—Margaret was the name she gave me—that he would be taken care of by his own daughter and her family, along with all of his friends. Still that was not enough for her to break me away, and as you know, I followed all of you to your cars. When you became lost Tom, I must admit that I shoved the door on your head, as I did not think that it was a benevolent outcome what had happened. Margaret was appalled. I did stay around for a while after that, but Margaret said it was time to go, so we left.

Did you notice any tone, music, lights, a tunnel . . . what?

The trip was very beautiful. As we rose into the sky you could see these brilliant lights all around with celestial music playing. I knew, but I didn't know, as I was still veiled.

Before we go into that, I have a question for you from Robert. As you probably know, he cannot find your diamond ring or the address book.

I want you to tell him how much I still care for him and love him. It was just my time to leave. I had that extra bonus year from the time of the car wreck, and it was filled with a lot of joy and pleasure.

I will pass that along. Can you tell me if the diamond ring is in your house?

Most definitely, Tom.

Is it in the bedroom?

It is not in the bedroom, Tom.

What about the bathroom?

No, not there either.

Kitchen?

Yes. Have him search the drawers there.

I'm surprised you did not put the ring in your bedroom, Joy.

It was a last minute decision. I had to run out the door, so I slipped it off and placed it in a drawer for safekeeping until I returned.

Where did Robert put the address book?

Oh, he will find these with a little more searching Tom. They are in some of the clothes he wore. In a pocket.

He was quite stunned by your passing, Joy, so I'm sure you can understand his mindset at this time.

Of course I do.

So back to your arrival. Where did you arrive?

It was a beautiful setting, Tom. It was just as I have always envisioned it to be. That's the key, you know. It's what you want it to be—grand vistas or an intimate setting, a building, gates, a beautiful forest, whatever will make you the most comfortable.

Who was there to meet you?

My first husband, as you can imagine, plus other relatives that passed over before me, a few cats and a few friends who I knew in this life. It was a very joyful celebration—a great reunion, as these things go. It makes the transition that much easier.

Then where did you go?

I was taken by Margaret to a pleasant place—a cottage. That's where my soul group started taking over for Margaret and she said goodbye. This is where I've been for some time, resting after a long life with the many challenges I gave myself. Now I will start my planning for my next life while still keeping a fragment of myself around Robert and my daughter so that I can continue to assist them in their lives. I still have those connections, and I will have them until they all pass over themselves. But I'll be there at your New Year's party and will be sending all of you my energy and light. I know you will all take care of Robert, and I'll act as one of his guides.

I guess that's all the questions I have for the moment. I hope I received most of what you told me.

Yes, I think you did. And I do apologize for my impulsive action at the car. I could not see the larger picture, as I'm able to see it now. I lashed out at you for that reason.

Apology quite accepted, and later, as you know, I laughed about it, as we all know how feisty you were in life. That made you a special friend. I do wish you a good life, and perhaps we will speak again one day, if I've forgotten to ask something, or to improve my reception.

You will continue to improve. I know that you will contact Robert for me and tell him how very much I still love him. Tell him that we will have other lives together. He hasn't gotten rid of me yet.

All my love, Joy.

☀   ☀   ☀

I spoke with Joy again on December 23, 2008.

Joy, you mentioned your duties in respect to this past life. What would those consist of?

Yes, Tom. I do have some duties. First, I know you were going to ask me about reviewing my life, and yes, we have done that. It really does not take that long on this side of the veil.

With whom did you do that?

With my soul group. We are very close and supportive of one another. And my soul itself is there to share. There are no real judgments that are made. We review the soul contract and the changes that I made during my life. It's in a way very complicated, but it's really not—not on this side.

Are there any other duties you need to do?

Yes. I need to give some comfort to Robert during his grieving period, and to my daughter and family. I know you were going to ask me about the Memorial Service in January, and I wouldn't miss that, now could I?

No. You'll hear only good things said about you. How many lives have you lived on Earth now, Joy?

A few hundred—I'm not a really old soul, but I'm moving along, shall we say. The number is around 452. Yes. That is close.

Is there some reason Robert cannot communicate with you in meditation?

Yes, Tom. He is blocking my attempts to speak with him. Tell him he needs to relax more and have a notebook to write down any impressions and words that he might think, as those will be from me. Tell him to relax more. He can do it if he doesn't try too hard.

I will pass that along. He has searched for the diamond and the address book and has not found either one. Did I incorrectly receive their location, or do we just need to narrow it down?

You need to narrow it down a little. You did not receive the information incorrectly. The diamond is in the kitchen in a drawer, almost in plain sight.

Is it near the sink or on the island?

Nearer the sink. He'll see it even if he has to take out all the items in the drawer.

What about the notebook?

That may be a little more difficult for him. It was in a pocket, and now it may be lying on the floor among some clothes. He will find it eventually.

Did you buy a Christmas present for him?

No. I thought I had time to buy one. When I told him I had finished my shopping, I meant for the relatives. He was next on my list.

Now I wish I had, but such is life. Please tell him my love for him is his Christmas present, and it will be there for all the Christmases yet to come in his life. Love is so much more than a present, and I think he'll understand that too. It is everlasting love.

Thank you, Joy. I must go now. I wish you a good life and a great next one too. See you at the New Year's party.

✳   ✳   ✳

A couple of notes: I decided that this would be the last time I would contact Joy, as the soul I was speaking to I could feel was no longer the personality we knew of as Joy. Robert did find the address book, but in a pile of papers, not clothes, and he still hasn't found the ring. Either I did not receive this properly—although I asked several times—or he just hasn't looked in the right drawer yet. Maybe finding something like the ring is supposed to come through inspiration—that whisper in your ear, as Theo calls it. Robert was eventually able to communicate directly with Joy.

CHAPTER NINE

BENEVOLENT OUTCOMES FOR BUSINESS TRAVEL

I travel to Cannes, France, every April and October for a world television and video market. In the years since my first book was published, I have requested many benevolent outcomes on those trips, so I'll relate more of those stories here, along with many others sent to me from all over the world.

My daughter and I were headed for Cannes one April. My French buddy Dominique, who lives in Park City, Utah (and specializes in sales to France), left for France a week earlier than my daughter and I did in order to meet with his clients in Paris. From Paris he traveled by train to visit his grown children in Lyon, which is the second largest city in France and is located between Paris and Cannes. When it was time to take the high-speed train down to Cannes, he looked in his luggage for the roundtrip ticket, and it was not to be found! He looked everywhere, and finally he requested a benevolent outcome to find the ticket, as it was worth 250 Euros (over $300). At the train station, he went to an office to replace the ticket, as he had paid by credit card. They refused to replace it and sent him (he was steaming by this time) to another office, to repurchase the ticket. At that office, he was informed that a homeless person had found his ticket in the train station and had tried to cash it in, but they refused, so they gave him his ticket back!

When my daughter and I flew to Paris on Continental from Houston, the plane had a mechanical problem in the cockpit, so we were delayed in departing and arrived too late for our connection to Nice on Air France. We stood by for the next flight, but it was full. The next flight that was open was not until after nine that evening. The Air France people suggested that we take the shuttle bus across Paris to the airport in Orly and board a flight there. We agreed, but they said we would have to have our bags pulled and brought to the baggage claim area. After waiting for an hour, they finally told us they would send them down on the next plane. We were so short on time that we took a taxi, requesting a most benevolent outcome to arrive on time for the flight, as it would be close. We arrived only twenty-five minutes before the flight, but because we had our boarding passes, we were able to make it to the gate just in time. Naturally, our bags were not there in Nice, so we filled out lost-baggage forms, and I asked for another most benevolent outcome for them to arrive safely. They were delivered the next day while we were at lunch on the sunny Cannes beach.

During these markets, I always request benevolent outcomes at the start of the day and at other times for all my business meetings. I find that the meetings run more smoothly, and the results are better. I have had representatives from companies that we did not have appointments with walk up to the booth or into our business suite at a market and want to do significant business with us. These are always very pleasant surprises.

I normally use mileage on an airline to upgrade from coach to business class. Most of the time, I'm confirmed about one month before departure, but on this trip, I was confirmed only for the trip over and not back. I asked for a benevolent outcome that both my daughter and I would be upgraded on our return, but the flight had been sold out and there would be no upgrade. What did happen, though, was when the door closed in the sold-out coach section, there were two seats left open in the row just in front of us. I quickly suggested to the lady in our row that she move to the window seat in the next row. This gave both rows a seat in between. We were the only two rows with an empty seat, making the trip a little more comfortable.

For Taxis

You can also request MBOs for a short taxi or rental-car line. At the Las Vegas airport this past July, we were in what seemed to be a very short line, so I asked a police officer about it. He said the line would be tripled or quadrupled within the next fifteen to thirty minutes. The benevolent outcome was a lull in the number of people lining up for taxis. Don't forget to request an MBO for an honest taxi driver, plus a safe trip to your hotel. Taxis can break down or be involved in wrecks, so you want to cover that possibility before even getting in line. The request for a short line, an honest driver and a safe trip to your hotel can all be said at one time. Just say, "I request a most benevolent outcome for a short taxi line, an honest taxi driver and a safe trip to our hotel. Thank you." If you're in a city and on the street in need of a taxi, request a benevolent outcome for a taxi arriving "soon," "quickly," "in three or four minutes," or however you wish to word the request.

In Dangerous Cities

Some cities in the world are just more dangerous than others. When you go out, request a benevolent outcome for your walk or drive from point A to point B. In Barcelona last year, the first thing the front desk told me upon checking in was to watch out for pickpockets when I went out for dinner. When you are driving, request an MBO for the drive and a parking space when you arrive. If you have driven in Europe, you know that car break-ins and thefts are just a fact of life there. Request an MBO that your car remains safe and secure wherever you park it. I've been amazed at how many smashed car windows I've seen over the years in Europe, with the thieves after the radio. Manufacturers finally started making radios that could be easily removed by the driver.

One year, between markets in Cannes and Milan, a business colleague and I drove into Italy for a six-day vacation. The first night we stopped in Pisa so that we could visit the Leaning Tower the next day. The hotel was the largest in the city and had its own parking garage. We pulled in and, after putting our bags in our rooms, went three doors down for dinner. Before we had finished our dinner, the manager of the hotel came by and told us that a couple of drug addicts had broken into our car. We returned to the car and found that not just one window but three were smashed, as one of the thieves had cut himself and then taken it out on the car. I immediately requested a benevolent outcome for resolving the car problem. "Luckily," the exact same model of car was available at the local rental agency and we exchanged our vehicle for a new one. In Naples, car thefts were so bad that the hotel had us park in the police parking lot down the hill from their location.

At Cannes Again

I recently traveled to Cannes, again on my semiannual trip to an international television and video market held there. This was an uneventful trip (thanks to requesting most benevolent outcomes) with two exceptions: I had the little "whisper in my ear" from my guardian angel Theo in Frankfurt while waiting for my connection that my watch was going to stop working, and I remember thinking (I was foggy from being on a plane overnight) that at least it had lasted for twenty years. Then I awoke from a nap while waiting and discovered the watch had stopped, and it was only twenty-five minutes until boarding time.

Upon arrival in Cannes, I headed for the Rolex store nearby to see if it could be fixed (after requesting an MBO). I was having a hard time finding the address and stopped in another watch store to ask directions. After finding the store a few doors down, I was told it would take four to six weeks and a minimum of 400 to 600 Euros ($600 to $900) for the repair. I know prices in the U.S. are lower, so I headed back to the other store and bought the least expensive watch they had to tide me over until my watch was repaired. Had I not stopped in for directions, I would not have known where to go for a less expensive watch—a nice benevolent outcome!

The next night I ate at a pizza and Italian food restaurant near the old port in Cannes. There are a lot of these in the area, as Italy is just an hour drive or so away, just past Monte Carlo. I pulled my reading glasses out of the case and the lens on the left side, along with the screw, dropped out on the table. The screw rolled off the table and even with two waiters assisting me, we couldn't find it. I requested a benevolent outcome and luckily the print on the menu was large enough to read.

This morning I asked the front desk where to have the glasses repaired and was advised there was a store only one block away. The repairperson replaced the screw and even the pads, which she said were yellow, and at no charge! It was a nice MBO. I do know, from similar things happening like this before, that I set these little challenges up on a higher self level in order to force me out of my routine, which also allows me to speak French; I am only able to use my French two times a year now. I used to also attend the Cannes Film Festival, but my lower-budgeted regional films didn't sell well there, as that is a market for art films and for films with highly recognizable stars, so I stopped attending.

At the Italian restaurant I mentioned above, I requested an MBO to sit next to someone interesting, knowing that a lot of my colleagues were arriving for the market. When I arrived, I was seated at a table by the wall with empty tables next to me. After my experience with my glasses, two young ladies came in to eat and instead of sitting one table away from me, sat down next to me. We started talking and they were from Toronto, Canada, and also there for the television market. The talk eventually led to a discussion about benevolent outcomes and one of the ladies, named Jenna, said that her mother had just returned from Sedona! Jenna and her friend Valerie said they would try asking for benevolent outcomes in their meetings. A couple of days later I received an email from Jenna saying that the requests were going great.

I also went to a PBS reception in a penthouse that overlooks the whole bay of Cannes. I again requested an MBO to talk to someone interesting, and there were plenty of interesting people there. I eventually went to dinner with five ladies, mostly in South American sales and television broadcasting. One of the ladies said she was going to put me in touch with her dubbing service in Argentina, and she would tell them to give me the same rate she has. Another of the ladies was interested in some of my documentaries for their television channel. These are just two examples of how many ways there are to request benevolent outcomes in your work and life. Make it a habit!

Yet Another Trip to Cannes

I took another of my twice-a-year trips to Cannes, France, for the world television market this past March. This time I stopped over in England to do the first international workshop for my first book. I requested a large number of MBOs during the trip. I now always request MBOs for the safe arrival of my luggage, for getting through the security line with no problems and for sitting next to an interesting person on the plane. I always travel business class if I have enough mileage to upgrade, and on the Continental flight from Houston to London, I did just that. The plane was not full, and there was no one next to me. That allowed me to spread out, with my things in the seat next to me, and I went to sleep after taking a melatonin (a vitamin that helps you sleep, if you are not familiar with the name). Plus it was easy getting up to go to the restroom without having to climb over someone else in the middle of the night.

I requested an MBO to easily find my sponsor (Val Stoner of *Ahh* e-zine) at the London Heathrow Airport, and I stood waiting at the coffee shop for less than five minutes when she arrived. She had arranged for me to have the largest room at a very nice bed and breakfast in Henley-on-Thames. The bed and breakfast was only a one-block walk to the railway station, and on Thursday I went to Windsor for lunch with one of my DVD company clients from the UK.

I had to change trains twice and requested MBOs for getting to the right train. At each of the two stops there were kind people who directed me to the correct track. I even sat near a gentleman from Philadelphia who was a head-hunter (someone who works for a job-placement service) living in Windsor and a lady going to a play who was headed for the West End in London. They directed me to Don Beni's Restaurant—the waiters sing there; it's a fun place if you are ever in Windsor visiting the castle. On the way back I was okay with the first change, but arriving in Twyford, I wound up following a sign that said Henley, but was incorrect. There was no one on that platform to ask. Then suddenly out of nowhere two ladies appeared, inspecting some construction work on the platform. I asked for help and they said that the train was on a different platform, then pointed to the train already sitting there. I thanked them and ran up the stairs, over the bridge and down to the platform, thinking they might close the doors at any second. They didn't until three minutes after I entered the train car. Now that was a benevolent outcome!

We had a great time in the workshop, as I had requested an MBO for that, and I had everyone else request it too. Then on Sunday Val and her husband Jim took me to the London City Airport for the flight to Nice, France. I naturally requested an MBO for the drive, as we had to go through the middle of London. We arrived in plenty of time. I really must publicly thank Val for all her work and friendship. She's a great lady and a catalyst for benevolent change in the United Kingdom. Mine was the first workshop she arranged in the UK, but she has several more in the works. There's already talk of me returning to Henley. If there's anyone else who would like to sponsor a workshop, let me know, as I must plan months in advance.

The London City Airport is such a small airport that they close the security line down at times. Naturally I requested an MBO for my luggage to arrive on time and for my trip through the security checks to go smoothly. I also requested an MBO to sit next to someone interesting on the plane. The Air France commuter jet I flew on held eighty-one people, and it was stuffed with folks attending the world television market I was headed for. There was a jolly English chap who sat on my row in the plane and we exchanged business cards. He's the managing director of an Internet supply company and upon my return had already sent me an email suggesting we do some business. The London City runway is so short that the pilot kept the brakes on while revving the two jet engines up to full power, then let off the brakes—and off we went like a catapult.

Our arrival in Nice was in a downpour. I had been given a free bus pass as part of my platinum card service, earned through many years of attendance at this market, so I requested an MBO to not have to wait too long after I picked up my luggage. The wait was a short ten minutes. Again there were lots of market people on the bus to talk to. As it was raining, I hurriedly walked the two blocks to my hotel with an umbrella stuck in my jacket while I rolled my two bags.

After checking in, I requested an MBO to pick up my badge with no problems, and that went smoothly—with no lines. I had requested an MBO for someone interesting to sit next to for dinner, and it turned out to be my old friend Dominique, as a dinner with a French client had been cancelled when the client decided not to attend at the last minute. It was nice to catch up, as I know that having these dinners will not happen as often in the future; Theo has told me that our paths will divide more in the future, especially when requesting benevolent outcomes becomes widely known in the next couple of years.

Each day at the market, as I do every day, I would say the "expect great things today" mantra, and then I would request an MBO for all the meetings that day to be productive and the results to be even better than I could hope for or expect.

I won't bore you with the rest of the details of the business portion. I requested MBOs for not having to wait long for the bus back to the Nice Airport and it was again less than a ten-minute wait. I was hoping for an upgrade to business class for the flight to Paris, but it was all coach. The MBO was that I was able to get into the elite or business class line so my wait was much shorter than the coach line, and two of my clients from Japan were in line. They got me an invitation to the elite lounge where I had a free sandwich and cola.

In Paris, my bag showed up in reasonable time and the wait for the shuttle bus to the hotel was not too long. I flew back to Houston on Air France the next morning next to an attorney whose main client in Europe was Airbus, and he was pleasant. On the plane I mentioned just a little about *The Gentle Way*. Upon deplaning, as we approached passport control, there was a huge crowd there from two 747s that had arrived just before us. As we went through the queue, I saw there were two lanes that were roped off. I quickly requested an MBO for them to open, and they did open just three people in front of me. I told the attorney that this was an example of *The Gentle Way*. The rest of the trip was uneventful—a nice MBO!

TIMESHARE DEAL

By the time you read this, I will have had two workshops on my book in Braintree, Massachusetts and one in Andover, Massachusetts. As neither I nor my wife have ever toured that section of the country, I thought it would be nice to find a place to stay on Cape Cod in between the two workshops, so I requested an MBO that we could trade one of the time shares we own (another MBO where we bartered some movies for broadcast on a Utah TV station) for a time share on Cape Cod. There was a long waiting list on RCI.com, so I checked out craigslist for Cape Cod weekly rentals, and there were quite a few. I thought it best to wait until the first of August to try and trade for a cottage on the Cape, as I thought people would want to try and rent first before trading.

In the meantime, I was attempting to license my producer's Michael Jackson documentary to a U.S. DVD company whose owner I had known for many years. He happened to mention that he was flying to Boston for a week at his Cape Cod house, and naturally I brought up trading him the timeshare. I requested an MBO, and he came back saying that they were still going to be there on the week I needed. That proved to be fortunate, as their house is located a one-and-one-half hour drive from Braintree—not very convenient.

Then one day last week I had the "feeling" to check craigslist again and noticed that they had a trading section. There were a few trades listed for weekly rentals—some New Yorkers looking to trade their apartment for a week on Cape Cod, as an example. Most were for permanent trades. I decided to try a listing myself and listed it at 6:20 PM and requested an MBO. At 7:15 AM the next morning I had an email offering me a three-bedroom cottage in West Yarmouth, only a three-minute walk to the beach and harbor and quite close to the ferries to Martha's Vineyard and Nantucket islands. There was only one major problem—he had a specific request—a week anywhere in Hawaii for Christmas week. I found one studio listed on RCI, but by the time I prepared and sent a contract to him, it was already taken. I called and said I regretted we couldn't do it and resigned myself to starting calls around August 1.

He then telephoned me the next day and said that someone wanted to rent his cottage beginning on Friday, September 4 for a week (normally it was Saturday to Saturday), and he would be willing to do the deal if we could leave by noon on that Friday. He would wait to see if anything popped up again in Hawaii, but if not, we would find somewhere else to go next year. We were already planning to head for Andover that morning at 8:00 AM, as it's around a three-hour drive. I was not looking forward to checking RCI every two or three days until December, but then another MBO occurred when I checked RCI again: a one bedroom had opened up right on the beach on Maui—and a day earlier, which was perfect for his travel plans—so it was benevolent for both parties, which is one of the rules of requesting MBOs: that it be benevolent for all parties concerned!

As you look at the twists and turns this took, you can see how it illustrates one of the points I mention in my workshops: It's great fun to watch the pieces come together for a benevolent outcome request, as you become more aware of what is taking place around you. You can use the analogy of a chess game where pieces have to be moved around the board. In this case it required my guardian angel to first locate someone to trade with me (instantly on their side, of course), then find someone who wanted to rent on a Friday-to-Friday basis over the Labor Day holiday and finally someone to give up a condo in Hawaii at the same time for the Christmas holiday, just as I searched. Again, it was great fun to watch all of this unfold!

CHAPTER TEN

BENEVOLENT OUTCOMES FOR VACATIONS

J ean from Ontario, Canada, was in Seattle vacationing in late February. I'll let her tell the story.

From Jean: "I was anticipating an afternoon of exploration via the excellent Seattle bus service. My destination required a transfer in downtown Seattle, and as I waited for my bus in the outlying area, I asked for a benevolent outcome for my ride to the downtown as well as for my transfer to a bus I'd not ridden before. As the driver approached his stop in front of the Seattle Center, home of the Space Needle, a parcel delivery truck suddenly stopped in front of him. The driver was not looking at the truck; he was looking at the bus stop to see if there were any passengers waiting. 'Something' told him to look ahead, and he did, bringing the bus safely to a stop within inches of the truck.

"There were about a dozen other people on the bus at the time, plus the driver. No one was injured; some of the people at the back didn't even know what had happened. But I did. (Thank you times ten!) I teased the driver about all the paper-work he had just avoided! We got to the downtown in plenty

of time for me to make my transfer, and I had a wonderful afternoon exploring the northern suburbs of Seattle."

———————➤-◦-⬟————————

Please note a couple of points from Jean's story. She was
aware of what happened when the bus driver was able to avoid
a collision with the truck. Instead of being frightened by the
experience, she was able to make a joke about it. I've seen
this several times before, in both my experiences and those of
others. You're able to step back and see a larger picture of the
events that go on to bring about a benevolent outcome. And
Jean also noticed that this was a radiant effect, which I have
written about previously, where a benevolent outcome that you
requested is given to you, and others who are nearby are also
benevolently affected.

Jean continues with her story: "Although my return trip
didn't involve the radiant effect, I was delighted with it as well.
I'd noticed that the bus back to the downtown ran only every
half-hour and cut it a bit short to walk back to the bus stop. As
I was hurrying up the hill, I noticed my bus signaling for its left
turn to get to the stop. I was still half a block away, so I hurried
even faster and began waving to the driver. He pulled into the
bus stop and waited for me. I got to the downtown transfer area
in lots of time to get my bus home, without a lengthy wait."

Meeting People and Ease with Airport Security

This next one you could call a vacation for a medical procedure. David in St. Louis sent me a couple of stories about a

trip he and his wife traveled to Cape Town, South Africa, for *in vitro* fertilization treatments, which are one-fourth of what they cost in the United States with as good, if not better, health care. He asked for a most benevolent outcome to meet people of like mind while on the trip. The manager of the bed and breakfast they stayed at was one of the organizers of the Earth-Water-Fire-Air Festival there in 2005. She also introduced them to one of her good friends, who was spiritually attuned and spent a night sharing wisdom.

Next David related: "I had to extend my stay down there. Fine, but when I went to change my ticket to a date a week later, it turned out that there were no flights available for the next two weeks. And the only option at the time was to spend an additional $2,600 for a new ticket. So as I prepared for the financial sting, I had a revelation: I was going to ask for a most benevolent outcome. Two days later, my travel agent called me saying that if I extend my stay by one and one-half days, I could use my original ticket and just pay the ticket change fee, which was $200. Wow!

"When it came time for me to leave, I asked for a most benevolent outcome for meeting the right people for my growth on the plane. So for one flight, I sat next to a very interesting woman who was director of a couple of burn units at some Cape Town hospitals. We talked at length about South Africa politics, social uplifting, tribal matters and so on, and it was extremely educational. I also met a very cool lawyer on the way home, who, in addition to being Jewish (I invited him over for Shabbat), was a social activist. He shared some wisdom and answered all of my questions about getting involved in social causes." [David explained to me that a

Shabbat is a sort of potluck dinner they have on Friday night. Sounds like good times with good friends to me!]

David also related a story about his recent trip to Israel on business: "Being a bit concerned about making it through today's airport security checks without a problem, I requested a most benevolent outcome for making it through security easily. I was in the very long line heading into the international gate area at JFK, and when I got to the point where they verify your boarding pass, there were two lines: one for commoners like me, which traversed back and forth about six times, and another for flight attendants that went straight through. Well, just as the person ahead of me and everyone ahead of her were directed into the maze, the gatekeeper closed off that path and let me be the first of the commoners to take the fast-path route through security. That was cool!"

━━━➣·❄·➣━━━

After reading David's email, my first chance to try out requesting an MBO for sitting next to someone interesting was my trip to Washington, DC, to promote my book at the largest book fair in the United States. On my way back I was flying economy class and the plane had two seats on one side and three on the other. I was on the window seat and a young lady came and sat down next to me. I thought, "Well, she doesn't look that interesting, but who knows?" Then another gentleman came and asked her if she wanted to switch places with him, as he had seen that she and her friend were separated. She immediately agreed.

I discovered that he was the head buyer for a chain of 150 bookstores, and I was able to present my book to him, later following up by phone, resulting in an order.

For Ski Trips

Here's an example of something that happened to me in February: I have a time-share in Park City, Utah, that I use each year to go skiing. This year, my son and I were going to leave on Friday, February 15 and fly up to Salt Lake City for a week of skiing. The Friday before departure I suddenly received an email from the resort company that manages the condominium complex; it stated that a retaining wall was in danger of collapse, and they had to cancel my reservation. Panic city! This is a very busy ski week—over the President's Day holiday—and I knew that Park City would be heavily booked. I immediately requested a most benevolent outcome (MBO) for the problem to be resolved. I picked up the phone and contacted the resort association. I was first offered a condo in Salt Lake City—a forty-five-minute drive over a mountain pass from Park City, then I was offered a condo at a smaller mountain, again about forty-five minutes from Park City and finally I was offered a condo about twenty minutes away. I said, "Keep looking," so the lady said that she would call Monday or Tuesday. I admit that I was worried, but I said, "I request a most benevolent outcome for a condo in Park City, and may it be even better than I can hope for or expect, thank you."

On Tuesday, she called and said that she had a studio condo in the same complex. They had obtained it from another resort company on trade, and it had not yet been rented. The only problem was that it was a Saturday through Saturday stay and not Friday through Friday. I requested another MBO when I called Delta to change my reservations. When I originally booked, I had to use one 100,000 miles for the two tickets, as the inexpensive 25,000-mile seats were already gone. When they checked on Saturday, the same flight was available, and for the Saturday return, an even better flight was available, and they were both 25,000-mile seats! I was able to redeposit 50,000 miles to my account for a future trip for $75 per ticket. Now that's what I call an "even better than I hope for or expect" result!

A Real Fish Story

Rachelle writes: "My husband and I had gone fishing, and we caught two catfish. They had swallowed the hook, and my husband had a hard time getting the hook out. I was not feeling good about the whole experience, so I asked for an MBO that any other fish we would catch be hooked in the lip so that we could remove the hook easily and set the fish free. I didn't want more than we could eat. Lo and behold! Every single fish we caught after that had the hook in the lip or corner of the mouth so it could be removed easily, and we put the fish back in the water. It made a most benevolent fishing experience! The fish and I were happy!"

Aha Moments

Some of you who are not requesting benevolent outcomes on a daily basis may not realize that your guardian angels constantly try to gain your attention and let you know they are there. I'm sure that you have heard people mention that whenever they look at a clock it invariably reads "11:11" or some other constant time. This may have happened to you too.

As I've had to travel a lot—first with our international wholesale tour company and then with our international film distribution business—I would always seem to wind up in rooms with five as the sum: 23, 32, 104, 203, 311, 401. When

I noticed, I would smile with recognition—ah, there Theo is again. Also, I've been recording my dreams every morning since 1979, and many times there would be some song that I had not thought of in a while that would be in my mind as I awoke. It was normally some love song. This came to mind as my son and I took a taxi to the DFW airport for our ski trip. The night before, for some reason I started thinking and then singing the old Bob Seger tune "Night Moves." This was a favorite of mine back in the years when I owned a convertible sports car. I would crank up the volume and sing along.

The taxi driver had picked us up once before, a tall guy with long, graying hair. He wasn't wearing a belt and had to constantly hitch up his jeans—sort of an aging hippie type. After we departed, he popped in a CD, and of course it was Bob Seger; and the last song we heard before he dropped us off at the airport was "Night Moves." Theo was saying hello again.

So watch for those aha moments. Your guardian angel is just reminding you that he or she is there. And if you've begun requesting benevolent outcomes on a daily basis, you'll be reminded every time that there is a loving being watching over you. This can happen hundreds and even thousands of times.

FLIGHTS AND TRAIN TRIPS

Annie in Ft. Lauderdale writes: "I just traveled to France and dreaded the flight. The planes are always very full and I usually never sleep for the nine hours they last. For my flight to Paris, I requested an upgrade of any kind. Well, I slept during half of the flight, which was a major improvement. I asked for a similar or better outcome for my flight back to Miami. This one is still amazing to me. The flight was far from full, with eighty-five empty seats. My daughter and I were able to enjoy four seats each, so we flew very comfortably and slept a lot. Even the crew had never experienced such an empty plane on that specific line.

"Another one for you: I had misread the time my high speed train (TGV) was leaving Aix-en-Provence by thirty minutes. I had told my older daughter, who was driving us to the station, that the train was scheduled to leave at 7:46 AM when in fact it was to depart at 7:16 AM. We left home at 6:55 AM for a drive that normally takes over twenty-five minutes. I asked for a time compression. We made it three minutes early, and the train was late by six minutes—something that never happens, as French trains have a reputation to run on exact schedule. Thank you so much for teaching the world about MBOs. I am planning on asking for bigger and bigger outcomes."

In Tuscany

Dianne writes: "Having introduced my sister-in-law Tracy to MBOs—and very successfully—she decided that obviously she needed to create an MBO for her family's journey from England on holiday to Tuscany, Italy. It's an arduous two-day journey, especially when there are two young children to keep amused!

"My brother-in-law called us on their arrival to say that they had experienced the smoothest journey yet (the family travels to Tuscany by car every year). They negotiated the tunnel between Switzerland and Italy (which is notorious for congestion) without the usual trouble and arrived at the vineyard hours ahead of time. My brother-in-law said, 'Tracy was doing those things you told her to do.' It took me a second or two to realize what he meant: MBOs, of course! And so MBOs continue to gain more supporters. How wonderful!"

May I also suggest for anyone to say, "I request a most benevolent outcome for this vacation, and may it be even better than I can hope for or expect, thank you!" That should allow your guardian angels to get really creative.

For Kids in Summer Camp

Julie writes: "My nine-year-old daughter was scheduled (and we paid) for a twelve-day overnight camp this summer. Then we decided to do a weekend family float trip. We scheduled a couple different dates, then settled on one it seemed everyone could make. The reservations were already in when I realized that it was the last weekend of my daughter's camping trip, which would mean either that she would miss the float, or we'd have to drive three hours one way to pick her up on the Friday morning we were leaving, and she'd miss the end of camp, which is usually a very good time.

"That same day I called the camp to see if she could switch from the second group to the first group two weeks before. I talked to someone who said she knew for sure that both camp trips were booked solid and had waiting lists, but that she wasn't the right person to talk to; I had to call back the next day. I got off the phone and immediately asked for an MBO, willing to accept whatever that might be.

"The next day I called and spoke to the right person. Amazingly she said she had just had a cancellation that morning and though both trips were still overbooked, the second trip was more overbooked than the first, so she would change my daughter to the first group right away. It actually made things better on her end too! Talk about an MBO for all concerned."

SUMMER CAMP UPDATE

Julie writes: "You might remember that I wrote you about an MBO for my daughter's camping trip: we had to change the dates to the first session because of a float trip planned, and even though both sessions were booked, the angels helped make that happen. Well, I now know another MBO that came out of that situation. All the campers that were there this week—which would have been the week she would have been there, if not for the MBO and changing the dates—went home sick with what might have been swine flu! It was all over the news! I thanked my angels profusely once again."

This is another example of not being able to see the full extent of what takes place when you request a benevolent outcome.

FOR FESTIVALS

Kelly writes: "I wanted to share a recent experience my family and I had regarding MBOs and parking spaces. My family is well aware of my frequent requesting of MBOs, as I do so in their presence at times. We were on a weekend vacation for Labor Day, in Madison, Wisconsin. A "Taste of Madison" festival was going on, and it is a college town, so needless to say, it was quite crowded. Students were returning to campus and a game was also taking place. Finding a parking place was trickier than usual for us as we got to town a bit later than expected. I immediately requested an MBO for a parking space with plenty of clearance, close to State Street and within the next fifteen minutes.

"We did find two spaces, but they didn't suit us because one had a meter that was broken—we didn't want to take the chance—and the other had a meter, only for us to realize we didn't have quarters! I had failed to be specific enough about that element. Our potential parking place did show up twice, but I didn't specify "not requiring coins." I remedied my request and asked for one in a parking garage we were just about to enter (others had been filled and I hoped that wasn't the case for this one). Sure enough, we found a nice spot with plenty of room around it and right off State Street in that garage. I thought it was worth mentioning this topic of a generally mundane parking spot MBO because it shows that specificity is important.

"Also, I wanted to mention to you that I state the benevolent prayer you have mentioned for diminishing karma daily. I find myself adding to the prayer where it states: 'I ask that any and all beings come to the aid and comfort of anyone that I have ever harmed either physically, mentally, morally, spiritually or emotionally. I ask that any and all beings come to the aid and comfort of any of the family members of anyone I've ever harmed in any way in any past, present or future life, and that the aid and comfort also go to any friends of those I've harmed.' So it would be 'family members and friends' in my rendition [this is the reader referenced in Chapter 7]. Is this something that is considered a good idea? I find, personally, that some of my friends are really more like family to me than my actual family members, thus my adding of those words. I was curious what you might think about this.

"My ten-year-old son has now begun stating MBO requests too, and he is amazed! He asked for it to rain for a whole day and it did. He didn't look at the weather forecast, either. He was tickled pink when it continued raining into the evening. (It gave him a break from watering the plants—his responsibility. The plants were happy too.) All the best to you!"

⸻⸻⸻◆⸻⸻⸻

Yes, when you request benevolent outcomes, they do have to be specific, as Kelly found out. Now why didn't I think to add family and friends to the daily benevolent prayer? Thanks, Kelly!

FOR AIR TRAVEL

Val writes: "I am now back in the UK (from the U.S.A.), and I thought you would like to know that before the flight back, I requested a most benevolent outcome, and guess what? My husband and I were upgraded to business class. We had a won-derful journey home."

Val also writes of another time: "I have just returned from Slovenia. To start, four of us were traveling together. I was the only one who had speedy boarding on this cheap airline flight. My friends said that the extra I had to pay was useless as they had traveled many times with this airline and loads of people pay for the privilege of getting on first. I did the usual requesting the MBO and surprise, surprise, there were only five of us boarding first—and guess what? I was able to get front row seats. One friend sat next to me and the other two got seats behind us.

"Coming back I did the same procedure, as there were five of us traveling together and this time there were many more people with speedy boarding. I was again allowed to board first and sat in the front row, and unbelievably, none of the seats around me got taken. So even though my friends were well down in the queue, we all sat together. Thank you so much for telling me about requesting MBOs."

Kathy in Seattle writes: "I'm so happy that I met you at the Kryon event in Sedona. Talk about an MBO! I had wanted to get your book, and there you were. I love buying books from the author and getting books signed right then and there. It makes it very special for me.

"I want to share an incredible MBO with you. As I was waiting in the airport for my plane I was reading your book. I thought I'd try an MBO, so I requested that I sit next to interesting people. I added fun, too. My seating section was called, and as I moved into line, I heard someone call my name. It was a dear, dear friend of mine whom I hadn't seen in months. She lives in a town about 1.5 hours drive from my home, so we don't get to see each other often. Unbelievably, she was on the same flight! She's a Unity minister and had been at a conference in Phoenix. Her ticket placed her about ten rows ahead of me in the plane.

"As I got seated, she came back to talk with me for a bit and the woman who was sitting in the aisle seat offered to trade places with her. I had the window seat, which meant that we'd be talking over the person in the middle. That person showed up and he turned out to be a very nice man who was more than willing to trade seats with me and get the window seat. Everyone had an MBO. I got to sit next to my friend and we had a delightful marathon conversation all the way to Seattle. The woman who had been in her seat got to get off the plane faster and also had more leg room because it was a bulkhead seat. And the man whose seat I traded with got a window seat.

"I'm having lots of fun with MBOs and am sharing them with anyone who will listen! Thanks for sharing the gentle way."

For Train Trips

Lorice in Fort Worth, Texas writes: "I have an MBO to share. I took the Amtrak train from Fort Worth to Joliet, Illinois, the stop right before Chicago, which was the end of the line. I asked for an MBO for a timely arrival of the train in the Fort Worth station and at my destination. Those trains can be really late, sometimes by three or four hours, which is why I requested the MBO. Well, on the trip up the train was only about one hour late in arriving in Joliet, and on the trip back down here we arrived early! This is the best time we've ever made on any of my train trips to Joliet."

For Rental Cars

Vicki in Texas writes: "My husband and I have had some good outcomes using MBOs. Most recently we used them when we were late to return a rental car. I requested an MBO so we could return the car and hopefully avoid late fees. It worked perfectly. We also use them a lot for matters surrounding health and home projects. We requested an MBO for a successful roof job, which worked great. With recent hurricanes, costs were high for roofing, and this simple project had many challenges. In the end we got the roof we wanted for a great price."

Driving Benevolent Outcome

Kathy in Washington writes: "I was driving from Seattle to Vancouver, B.C. to attend a workshop and a group twelve-strand DNA activation. There were several places I was going during my travels, including motels, houses and businesses. For my birthday, I'd received a Garmin GPS and was looking forward to the first real chance I'd have to use it.

"I'd carefully inserted all the addresses of these places in my Garmin and it had directed me, without error, to the Costco gas station in Bellingham. Next was my motel in a town near Vancouver. As I was driving along, it suddenly began flashing 'low battery.' No problem, I thought. I'll just plug it into the car charger. However, when I tried, the end that went into the Garmin kept falling out. I was beginning to panic. All my information for every one of my destinations was in my Garmin. I hadn't written them down anywhere. I turned it off to save what little battery was left, thinking I'd just turn it back on when I got into Canada.

"Before I hit the border, I stopped at a rest stop. I sat in my car for a few minutes thinking about my quandary and then remembered to ask for an MBO. I requested that I find the solution to the low battery problem quickly and easily. I used the facilities and came back to my car, thinking to try one more time to insert the car charger. When I picked up my Garmin, it happened to be upside down. It was then that I noticed the connection for the car charger. I'd been trying to plug it into the wrong place. Thank you angels. I continued on and it worked perfectly the entire week I was traveling."

For a Mexico Vacation

Lynn from Oregon writes: "My husband and I are going to Mexico in May to celebrate our thirtieth anniversary. We don't do much traveling. so this is big for us. We are going to Riviera Maya outside of Cancun. I asked for an MBO when planning this trip and got incredible prices—I trust it will be the perfect place for us to be staying!

"We will be going on a day trip to Chichen Itza, a place we both wanted to experience. So I am wondering if any of your guides know anything about this location and if there is a chance of having a spiritual experience there? We will of course ask for MBOs the whole trip!"

⇒⊶•⊷⇐

Theo, why do people feel strange when climbing the Chichen Itza pyramid in Mexico?

Yes, as you may have guessed, the stones have many energies imprinted on them from the past—both good and bad. The pyramid itself has energies from its geographic location and its situation in connection to the astrological alignments. So, between them all, you have a lot of energy that sensitive people can feel quite easily, and even less sensitive people can feel them to a certain extent as well. For anyone visiting Chichen Itza, do request an MBO to have an experience there at the pyramid.

For Housing Rentals

Charlene writes: "To add to your huge list of successful MBOs: I left it a bit late in making reservations for Memorial Weekend. We were combining a graduation ceremony with a couple days at the beach, and in Northern California it can be rather insane finding a little hideaway if not booked very early. So my request was to find a wonderful little cottage that didn't break my bank account and was within one hour of the beach and one hour of where we were to attend the graduation. Within two hours of looking online, I found the absolutely perfect place nestled in its own little redwood grove twenty minutes from the beach and about the same distance from where the graduation was going to be held. I continue to stand in utter awe and gratitude!"

Locked Out

Bonnie writes: "This past week we were in Arizona for my son's wedding. We rented a house in the area. Although we were given a key for the house, we never carried it with us. Instead, we used the keypad on the garage door and left the door inside to the house open, entering the house this way. However, one day, in my haste to get somewhere, I forgot and locked the door inside of the garage! When we returned and went through the garage, we found the door to get into the house locked. Panic set in immediately. We walked around the house but found no other possible way to get in. We did not have the owner's name or number with us, either. I immediately asked for an MBO to find a way into the house. Suddenly, my husband started looking at the locked door and pulled a credit card out of his wallet. Within ten seconds of trying to get the door to open, he did it! This door was a very solid, secured door. There is no doubt my guardian angel helped him get that door open, as my husband had never done anything like this before!"

Hotel Room Discount

Jaye writes: "I requested an MBO for my trip to Chicago, and it went very well! I had made a reservation at a hotel because I couldn't stay with my daughter, as she has cats and I am allergic to them. I went to check out this morning and told them that the bed was a bit hard to sleep on. They are in the process of remodeling, and so they gave me the $10 discount for reserving the room online plus another $64 because the bed was too hard. For three nights, with the room taxes and everything, it was only $219, as opposed to $284. My math may not be so good now, as I am fairly tired, but the upshot is that I got almost an entire night's stay for free!"

Can You Request Too Many MBOs?

Diana in Hong Kong writes: "My sister wants to ask whether it is possible to make too many MBO requests? (I don't think so). I think you and your guardian angel also said it in your first book, yes?

"I just came back from a trip to Shenzhen with our two young kids, and MBOs helped a lot during our vacation. On our way back, I didn't forget to request MBOs for passing through Chinese customs quickly and safely, and the car passed through quickly without a hitch. We got a friendly officer who liked children. And we seemed to safely get the best-looking taxis (in China the taxis tend to be pretty old)."

You can't request too many MBOs. That's just a third-dimensional idea. These guardian angels are so powerful that as I've said before my guardian angel could handle 10 million requests for a parking space at the same time and never break a sweat (again using 3D terminology). Remember that they are taking care of each of us in all of our lives on Earth all at the same time (600 to 800 lives—past, present and future—on average) and in all twelve timelines for each life, for all soul groups (6 to 12 on average per soul) for 6,000 to 19,000 souls on average. Do the math and that comes out to one billion or so decisions each minute! It's just beyond our third-dimensional understanding. I asked Theo about this.

———⊷∙◦∙⊶———

Are my figures correct about the 1 billion or more decisions you must make for all the soul fragments in all our lives being lived at the same time?

Yes, Tom, more or less. Perhaps I don't normally think of it in those 3D terms, but on your level of understanding, yes. I have millions of decisions and acts of assistance I provide to soul fragments in any given minute of all lives being lived at the same time. You just had no understanding until recently of exactly what I meant by multitasking, as it was beyond your ability to conceive it at that time. You will have even more of an understanding to look forward to in the future. So yes, those figures could be accurate, although naturally there are fluctuations.

So it sounds to me like Theo might have been nicely saying that I was a little high on the numbers. But as he says, he doesn't think in those 3D terms, and what exactly that means we'll leave alone for the time being.

CHAPTER ELEVEN

BENEVOLENT OUTCOMES FOR THE HOLIDAYS

The month of December is generally viewed as a great month of parties, dinners with friends and reunions with family. But it can also be a highly stressful time if you are in charge of dinner or have to travel, or if you and your family are worlds apart in terms of lifestyle and beliefs. I'm going to give you some tips and suggestions to make this time period much less stressful and a lot more pleasurable by requesting benevolent outcomes. You can request a benevolent outcome that your visit with your family or friends be cordial and pleasant. This may seem like you are asking a lot in some instances, but ask for the impossible!

Under this category comes family members or people you know will be at the party who you have a difficult time with because they are alcoholics or you have had a difficult relationship with them in the past. I suggest saying something like:

*"I ask that any and all beings come to the assistance
of (name) so that they remain sober and pleasant
during the time I'm there, and that they receive
assistance in overcoming their problem."*

This is a benevolent prayer that you can say for other people. Change the wording to fit your circumstances. If you are worried about your safety or your children's safety while in the presence of someone you know to be physically, mentally or sexually abusive, then say, "I ask that my safety and the safety of my children be guaranteed now and in the future in a way that is benevolent to us all." This also can be said if you are currently in a relationship in which you are fearful for the same reasons.

I have mentioned the radiant effect before, but remember, when you request benevolent outcomes for yourself, it also affects others—in this case, those who are at the dinner, party or reunion with you. It makes for a much more pleasant time for everyone.

AT CHRISTMASTIME

Amy in Scotia, New York writes: "I had great fun with a benevolent outcome on the weekend before Christmas. Because of bad weather in the East, my husband and I finally went out to find a Christmas tree on Saturday. I asked for an MBO, including finding the perfect tree quickly and at an even better price than I could imagine. We started out to a local grocery chain where they were selling trees, hoping to find a sale. On the way there, we ran across a long line of cars waiting for a light at a busy intersection.

"Sensing a message here, I turned the car around and headed back the way we'd come, going up a country road where we'd bought a tree from a farm stand in previous years. That place was closed, but up the road I saw a sign for Christmas trees. Walking in knee-deep snow, we found the trees and went to the door to get the proprietor, but no one was home. I shook the snow off one perfect tree and saw a price tag: $15!

"I took the money out of my wallet but wondered how I was going to leave it at the house with no one home. In my purse was an old paycheck envelope that I normally would have thrown away. Perfect. I wrote Merry Christmas on the envelope, put in the money and left it inside the front door. When was the last time you found the perfect Christmas tree for $15? I put it up yesterday and it's the most beautiful tree we've ever had. Happy Holidays to all."

Val from England writes: "Living in an apartment with very little storage, we have to be very selective about what we buy. I wanted to decorate the front pillar of our entrance with a Christmas tree. I only wanted to pay £5 because I knew I would just have to throw it away afterward. We looked in several garden centers, but all were over £25. Back in our hometown, the market was on, and lo and behold they had some lovely Christmas trees. Guess what? The one I wanted, which was nearly 6 feet tall, was just one penny under £5! The vender told me they were £40 in the shops, and I quite believed him. How blessed I was. Do you know, since you introduced me to MBOs, I do it automatically now—and amazing things come about."

A SON'S CHRISTMAS HOMECOMING

Marie writes: "Dear Tom, I have to thank you, the angels and God for the MBOs I received when I felt all was lost for my Marine son coming home to visit for Christmas. This morning my son was supposed to take a flight in from Washington. His flight was cancelled. Hearing there were some people waiting three days for a plane had me wondering if we would be able to spend any time with him, and I thought that if he didn't make it home, he had a good chance of being shipped out before I could see him. My son's dad and I started doing searches of the Greyhound bus service, since there was a flight available to a hilly area seven hours away. We found out the road was closed due to snow conditions, so the Greyhound bus was out. My ex was about to leave to drive there and pick him up, but then that plane was also cancelled because the airport was snowed in. There was no way for my son to fly in until December 26—after Christmas. This was one of my few chances to cook for my family, as each year I am never sure how much time I'll actually have with them. I decided to seriously ask for an MBO, and as I waited for word, I made a wreath, the best I have ever made. Then came the call: My son was boarding a plane and would be home in two hours. I cried and thanked the angels. Many, many thanks, Tom."

SPREADING THE WORD

Lyn writes: "It's New Year's morning and I had to write to express my appreciation of and excitement about this wonderful, new and gentle approach to life. I always believed that angels were out there, but I never thought that I could have a relationship with them. It wasn't until a friend passed along the two chapters posted on your website that I started inviting the angels into my life, and incredible and easy miraculous living started to unfold.

"My daughter and I were taking a girls' weekend down to New York City, and I read the chapters out loud to her on our drive there. It would take too much space to tell you all the marvelous things that joyously fell into our laps, but I will mention that we got bumped up to the most expensive seats for the Radio City Music Hall Christmas Spectacular! After that weekend, I realized that life has a splendid, happy and simple addition: Our guardian angels are there for us.

"So many amazing things have happened, but let me tell you about the biggest one. One of my wonderful jobs is that of a pet nanny. I live in people's homes and care for their beloved pets while they are away. It was the Saturday after Christmas and I was living in a home with a Great Dane and a greyhound. I was also taking care of several cats belonging to two different families, and I was visiting the cats each twice a day. I was at the second home, feeding the cats, when I had that dreaded feeling of the stomach flu bug hitting me like a bolt out of the blue. I felt sicker and sicker, and I just barely made it back to the dogs' home. I wondered how the heck I was going to make it through the day with all the animals looking to me for their needs.

"I was going through my list of who to call. I needed to find someone who could at least take the dogs for their afternoon walk. It was then that I realized I needed to request an MBO! I had just gotten your book a few days earlier. I also remembered about the condensed time concept, and that's what I requested. Tom, it was profound! As I was lying on the bed and dozing off, I felt I was being rocked back and forth, and then I slowly awoke to feel the nausea go up and out of me. I sat up and felt fine. I was able to walk the dogs, finish cleaning the family's house, visit the cats again, pack up and head for home. I felt like you feel the day after you've had the flu. I had the twenty-four-hour bug in two hours.

"I have been telling absolutely everyone about *The Gentle Way*. At the hair salon yesterday, I created quite an audience! I would love to do a little class. I often teach feng shui at a local recreation center, and I think offering a small class there based on your book would be such a neat way to share it with lots of people. What are your thoughts on having someone like me facilitate a class? Thank you so much for hooking me up with my guardian angels! Life will never be the same."

For Lyn and anyone else out there who would like to facilitate a class on *The Gentle Way,* let me know and I can point you in the direction of some of the usual questions people ask about the book. Plus I can hook you up with my publisher so that everyone in the class can purchase a book as part of the class.

Lyn recently updated me about the results of the class. **Lyn writes:** "Requesting MBOs helped so much with moving last week. Things went really well—the intermittent rain showers ceased while we were loading and unloading. I invited anyone from our recent guardian angel class to come and share their experiences. Many wanted to, but it was a busy weekend with graduations and so on. However, two ladies came out— the two who were the most skeptical.

"They went on and on about how many lovely things had happened that week. The one who was most critical of the idea spoke of a lunch she'd had with a friend who was very negative and unhappy—the woman always dreaded meeting up with her. She requested an MBO for it to be pleasant and joyful for both of them, and she said it was the best time they'd ever had—her friend even bought her lunch!"

FOR HOLIDAY SHOPPING

Jean writes: "I had a grocery store MBO on the afternoon of Christmas Eve. I knew the stores would be crowded with last-minute shoppers, but I really needed a few items. Knowing that the lines could be long, I still requested an MBO for a short line. With only eight items in my cart, I was still about fifteen people back from the express check out. While chatting with the woman ahead of me, I noticed a woman waving near the head of the line, and decided to see why. I came to find out she was trying to signal to her son that they'd opened a second express line, but she couldn't catch his eye.

"So I told her that I hoped she didn't mind, but I was going to go through. One woman was having her groceries bagged, the next man in line had three items and I was next! Instead of a twenty minute wait, I was out of the store within five minutes, laughing all the way, as I still had another errand to run and now knew I'd get there before closing time. Of course, I didn't have far to walk to my car!"

―――――❖◦❖―――――

As I have mentioned many times, requesting benevolent outcomes makes even mundane tasks easier and less stressful.

CHAPTER TWELVE

PERSONAL FUN TIME

O ne weekend my buddy Bob invited me to join him on a group canoe trip ten miles down the Trinity River. This river runs around the downtown area of Dallas, passing under a couple of interstate highways, railroad trestles and through an urban hardwood forest. I requested a benevolent outcome for the trip, as I hadn't canoed since my son's days in the Boy Scouts. My old canoe skills came back to me pretty fast.

The river was up several feet, from torrential rains the day before, so there was a lot of brush and trash in the river. We had one narrow scrape that could have resulted in us being dumped in the river. A metal triangular knob was sticking out of the water, with brush about ten feet to the right of it. I tried to maneuver the canoe to pass in between, but the flow of the river took us sideways, right into the knob. Then another canoe, guided by John, the organizer of the trek, did the same thing, and they wound up broadside to us. We were able to stay upright against the knob instead of dipping into the river while John pulled away from us. Then we were able to extricate ourselves off the knob.

The one surprise most benevolent outcome that occurred on this river trip was that I discovered that John works with a production company that recently finished a two-hour documentary on the Cherokee Trail of Tears, where the Cherokee Nation was forced by President Andrew Jackson to move en masse to Oklahoma in 1838. I have since met with John and one of the owners of the company, and we are currently evaluating that program plus a couple of others as to their marketability for international distribution. Those surprises are always fun, as you have no idea what will result when you request a benevolent outcome.

IN THE HOT TUB

From Lynn in Oregon: "I have had so many wonderful MBOs happen, sometimes I am just in awe—I always say please and thank you. One of my favorites is hot tub nights. Our tub is out on our deck, and living on the northern coast, there are a lot of rainy nights. My husband and I go out to the tub just about every Friday through Sunday night. We spend about thirty minutes each time.

"Now, the chances of it raining, as you can imagine, are big. We had to give it up quite a few times during the first winters we lived here. Then I started using MBOs. I would ask for the sky to be dry above our hot tub between such and such times, requesting an hour. I would say that we have a lot less rainy nights than we did the first couple of winters we lived here when I did not ask for MBOs. I say it was almost a fifty-fifty chance of rain in the winter here. Now 95 percent of the time it is either clear or just a bit misty. It may be cloudy and cold, but we don't care about that. Thank you!

"I use MBOs daily for lots of little things. I find it seems to work best for the small things that just make life simpler and more pleasant. And I so often find that when it doesn't work, it turns out there is a good reason. Something even better happens. Now that I have your email address, I will remember them and send them to you more often. Thank you for your wonderful book and for sharing."

———•○•———

If you have read my first book, then you'll remember the chapter about the Alaskan cruise where the whole group of us asked for clear days for our shore excursions and each day was clear. It was great.

Sending Loving Energy

Kelly writes: "I wanted to let you know that I employed a variant of the technique you had mentioned in your first book about communicating with animals with good success. I am now in the north woods of Wisconsin where there is much wildlife. Each morning I run or bike very early, between 5:00 and 6:00 AM and I always encounter three to seven deer. In the past, the deer would run off quickly after noticing my approach. I tried sending pictures of positive energy flowing out of me (not the photos of what I do during the day as you suggested with pets). I just imagine love, love, love, admiration and only peaceful intent. I noticed that when I did this, the deer wouldn't move away. One even walked in my direction closer after noticing me. One mother deer and two fawns stood unflinching, looking at me. Several of these deer were even on the edge of the blacktop I ran on and they didn't move. I suppose the communication came through and they sensed that my intent was free of danger.

"Another incident occurred yesterday as I was nearing the completion of my run. I had about a half a mile to go when I noticed a mother black bear with a cub following her across the road about seventy feet ahead of me. I grew nervous. I had never encountered a bear while solo and on foot in the thirty-four years I had been coming to this area. I do recall that on the outset of my run I had requested an MBO for a safe and comfortable journey, however. I stopped and ran in place saying under my breath, "help me please, help me please," over and over, wondering if a car might come up and pass me, sending the bears off running so I could pass comfortably. My concern was that no car would come since I was out so early, and most mornings not a single car passed me. About two minutes later, two cars came by from different directions and I was then clear to run past (the bears had since ambled off, but I don't know how far off the road they were. Of course I said a big thank you!

"Now, since my son missed the bear sighting, he is attempting to use a technique of sending visual images and positive loving intention for a bear to make an appearance for him. We'll see how that goes! From what I understand, animals can sense our intent and, as you said, they communicate through pictures. I'll keep you posted."

<hr>

In a *Sedona Journal of Emergence!* article, Robert Shapiro channeled an ET who discussed this very subject of sending animals loving energy [*Animal Souls Speak, ET Visitors 2*]. The ET said that animals will stop, pause and look back at you. So for the past couple of days when I encountered a rabbit that likes our front yard, I did just that. It works well. The only problem was this morning when we walked the dogs and he was out by the sidewalk and didn't want to move. I had to take my smallest dog (on a leash) and move up the sidewalk toward him to finally get him to move to the next yard and away from our other dog, who would have made short work of the rabbit.

A Benevolent Dinner

Ruth writes: "I am new to the practice of requesting MBOs. I shared the idea with a friend of mine as we were preparing to go out to dinner, and the two of us verbalized our request for an MBO for an enjoyable dinner out in a city new to both of us.

"We drove to a restaurant we thought we would like after determining that we wanted Japanese food and headed to a strip mall where we had seen one earlier in the day. As we maneuvered our way through the parking lot, a movie-dinner restaurant in the very back of the mall caught our eye. We parked at the Japanese restaurant and went in, only to find it crowded, noisy and so dark that the waitress gave us a mini-flashlight to read the menu. We ordered drinks, and while waiting for them, I excused myself and walked over to the movie-dinner house to inquire about it.

"It turned out to be a limited-seating, reservations-only place for dinner where a movie is shown during the meal. The evening movie was a recent Academy Award nominee that neither of us had seen. The movie would be shown within forty minutes. I took the last reservation available and skipped back over to the Japanese restaurant, where my friend was pleased with the idea. We ordered an appetizer to satisfy our desire for Japanese food, finished our drink and headed over to the movie-dinner theatre where we enjoyed a quiet meal and a wonderful movie.

"The MBO we jointly requested was better than we could have imagined. Furthermore, since you are in the movie distribution business, maybe someone out there might like the idea of this dinner theatre so that more of them can be made available—particularly to mature audiences. My practice of requesting an MBO is definitely going to become a new habit."

In Chicago

Paula wrote, "It worked—it really worked! I went to Chicago yesterday, and I did the driving from my sleepy little town 120 miles south of the Chicago area. I went to the mind, body and spirit expo in Northlake. Before I left I made a benevolent request for a safe trip, and then I was on my way with my best friend Beckie.

"The trip was exceptional with no traffic delays, and would you believe we found a parking spot close to the front door? I was dismayed when we got there because it was wall-to-wall cars and as we started cruising to look for a parking spot toward the back of the building, a car backed up to leave. I was amazed!

"When we left several hours later, we were counting our change to make sure we had the correct amount to make it through the tolls. My GPS said to take a right turn and Beckie said take a left. I figured she knew the way, but she had misunderstood the GPS and soon we were helplessly lost. The GPS told me to take another right. Have you ever tried to figure out which right when in the Chicago area?

"Anyway, when I finally took the assumed right, we had a wonderful drive, no tolls and little traffic—I found a neat place for our supper and got back onto route 55 in record time. I've always believed in angels and this was a wonderful way to verify their existence!"

CHAPTER THIRTEEN

BENEVOLENT OUTCOMES FOR RELATIONSHIPS

I n this chapter, you'll read stories about people looking for love and relationships, as well as stories from those wishing to benevolently separate.

REQUEST THE PERFECT MATE

Tracey writes: "I was told about MBOs and I've started saying them. I went to my son's boot camp graduation this past August. I said, 'I request a most benevolent outcome for meeting a great guy on this trip,' because I love military guys and I've been single for sixteen years. I'm hoping to get married soon. So I went to my son's graduation and met his master drill sergeant. And now for my birthday, which is September 26, he's sending for me to come and visit him. I'm requesting an MBO for this to be something very serious. Thanks for this information!"

━━━━◦❖◦━━━━

As I emailed back to Tracey, certainly you can say:

~~~~~~~~~~~~~~~~~~~~~~~~~~~~~~ *Benevolent Prayer* ~~~~~~~~~~~~~~~~~~~~~~~~~~~~~~~

"I request a most benevolent outcome for this
relationship to be serious and even better than
I hope for or expect, thank you!"

But at the same time, I suggest that she and all of you request an MBO for the perfect mate for you. If that drill sergeant is not the perfect one for her, it will end fairly quickly, but the request for the perfect mate allows her guardian angel to become involved, and it's not allowed to help her unless she requests assistance. That's very important to remember. Keep in mind that the Webster's Dictionary definition of "benevolent" is: "A kindly disposition to promote happiness and prosperity through good works, or by generosity in and pleasure of doing good works." That's exactly what your guardian angel wants to do for you, from mundane requests to serious ones like Tracey's—but you have to request their help.

YOUR LOVE LIFE

Maureen writes: "Tom, can I ask you something on a personal level? Someone I was in love with abruptly left me in early November. I have had a hard time letting go. I have asked for a most benevolent outcome to let go or to have the person come back. I also have asked daily for the right person to appear. I am so tired of being alone. I am a loving, kind and giving person; I do know how to love and care for myself, but this aspect is missing. I seem to have someone who comes close, and then he backs away. I am once again spending a weekend alone. I talk to my angels and pray, but nothing seems to happen. I do not know what else I must do. However, for small requests I have had a lot of proof that my angel is there. If you have advice, please send it along. Thanks."

———

Let's take the spiritual first, and then the practical. For those of you who have had a difficult personal relationship of any kind, you say:

Most Benevolent Outcome

"I request a most benevolent outcome for severing any energy cords that are no longer of benefit to me in a most benevolent way, thank you!"

Then of course you say:

Most Benevolent Outcome

"I request a most benevolent outcome for the perfect mate for me, thank you!"

Then each time you go out to the store, or any other activity, you say:

Most Benevolent Outcome

"I request a most benevolent outcome for meeting someone interesting today, thank you!"

Practically speaking, you can't sit at home waiting for that special someone to knock on your door. Start socializing. Both my daughter and her husband and two of our friends got together on the Internet. See what appeals to you and listen to that whisper in your ear. And volunteer in places where you might meet someone with similar interests.

Are there any clubs or organizations you can join? What about radio station get-togethers? When I operated my old singles ski club, a couple who met at my first party was married literally one month later. Many people have started long-term relationships after meeting at a party or on a ski trip. It even forced me to change the name of the ski club, as I was losing too many clients, so I opened it up to couples.

Ellen wrote that she had heard me on a radio broadcast, was lonely and wondered if asking for someone was a silly request. Here's how I responded: That's not a silly request. You would say:

Most Benevolent Outcome

"I request a most benevolent outcome for the perfect mate for me, thank you!"

Say it with some emotion and then sit back and watch things come together. And I don't mean sit in your house thinking love is going to walk in the door. I was just reading a Kryon channeling yesterday—hmm, now I know why!—from Lee Carroll (Lee's a super nice guy, as is his wife). In it, Kryon said that in order to create the seemingly magical synchronicity you wish, you have to open the door and get out and about. Find reasons to be out and meeting people—volunteer work, clubs and so on. Whatever that little whisper in your ear (as my guardian angel Theo calls it) says to do, listen and then do it. Then, when you think you've found someone interesting, say:

> "I request a most benevolent outcome that this relationship be benevolent for me, thank you!"

If it's not, then it will quickly end and you can continue until you find that perfect person.

FOR STRAINED FAMILY RELATIONSHIPS

Linda sent me a lengthy email about the very strained relationship she has had with her son since her divorce. She asked if there was anything she could do, so I asked Theo, and I felt his answer would apply to many readers in the same or similar situations. Theo, Linda in New York asks about her relationship with her son and any advice or perspective you can give to her.

Yes, Tom. She is having a difficult time. Of course it dates back to past lives when she rejected and did not care for her son, so she is having a balancing of karma in this life. She can each day send him beautiful, white, loving light at the start of her day. This will, over time, greatly assist her. She can also say the benevolent prayer that you say each morning [see Chapter 7], which will greatly reduce the karma. And finally she can request benevolent outcomes for each time she talks to him or meets with him that the results will be even better than she hopes or expects. Beyond that, she can explore those past lives so that she understands his rejection of her. With understanding, she can again send all her love to him.

Abusive Marriage

Connie writes: "I am having a hard time trying to figure out how to phrase an MBO. I am married with two young children. My husband is very aloof, unromantic and critical, and many times he is verbally abusive to me and my son. I feel that I should divorce him, except I know the children would be devastated by such an act. I am confused about what would be best for them under the circumstances. I have been working on my side of the issues for ten years and I am tired, depressed and even hopeless at times. Can you please suggest some MBOs for me?"

———◦———

For Connie and anyone else in this same situation, here's an excerpt from the Living Prayers chapter of my first book:

We all see and read stories about physical and sexual abuse in our communities, but there are those reading this book who are actually experiencing abuse on a daily basis. If you live in a household where there is verbal, emotional, physical or sexual abuse, you definitely should say:

Most Benevolent Outcome

> *"I ask for my safety and for the safety of my children be guaranteed now and in the future in a way that is benevolent for us all."*

If the reason for the abuse is because of an addiction to alcohol or drugs, you can say:

> *Most Benevolent Outcome*
>
> "I request that any and all beings come to the
> aid of (name) and assist (him or her) in the
> most benevolent way possible for our family."

Remember, you can ask for what seems impossible!

And I suggest that people in this situation see a marriage counselor on their own—and when you are choosing one, say:

> *Most Benevolent Outcome*
>
> "I request a most benevolent outcome for choosing
> the right marriage counselor for me, thank you!"

Then when you go to see this counselor, say:

> *Most Benevolent Outcome*
>
> "I request a most benevolent outcome for this
> session, and may the results be even better than
> I can hope for or expect, thank you!"

FOR DISSOLVING A MARRIAGE

Daphnee in Vienna, Austria, writes: "I read your newsletter with interest and there was a request about marriage in the last one. I am trying also to formulate an MBO so that my marriage dissolves without having to go through drama and trauma. Can you help me with a formulation that is more positive?"

For Daphnee and anyone else going through a divorce right now, I would suggest:

> *Most Benevolent Outcome*
>
> *"I request a most benevolent outcome for dissolving my marriage in the most benevolent way possible and ask that the emotional cords that are connected to my spouse be severed in a most benevolent manner, thank you!"*

Then you can also say a benevolent prayer for you and your husband:

> *Benevolent Prayer*
>
> *"I ask that any and all beings assist and comfort both my husband and me so that this divorce be as amicable as possible, and may the results be even better than we can hope for or expect, thank you!"*

I hope this eases the process for any reader in the same situation. Daphnee sent another email to me to update me on her situation: **Daphnee writes:** "Thank you so much for your MBO. It worked marvelously, at least the first step. In mid-February, as he was moving out, my husband informed me that he would not get a divorce. After I said the MBO and talked to God, this Saturday he called and asked me for a divorce. I will continue saying the MBO so that there is no quarrel between us and that the divorce goes through smoothly in divine timing and in divine ways. I will continue to keep you informed. Bless you."

CHAPTER FOURTEEN

BENEVOLENT OUTCOMES FOR GAMES OF CHANCE

I n my first book I noted that there are some of you out there who, due to your beliefs, do not believe in any form of gambling or games of chance in any form. If that's the case for you, then you can skip this chapter. As I said in the first book, I wrote the book for all faiths and beliefs.

EYES ON THE PRIZE

Lisa writes: "My most recent benevolent outcome worked. I was looking everywhere for your email address and couldn't find it. When I clicked on 'contact' on your site, I couldn't get it to work on my computer. I asked my guardian angel for an MBO to be able to find your email address so I could write to you. I had a feeling to check your site today, and there it was!

"I just had a few questions for you, if you don't mind. My first question revolves around winnings for raffles, prizes and so on. In your book, I believe your son really wanted to win a Playstation, and he did after requesting a benevolent outcome. What specifically would someone say when requesting to win a prize? I like to enter sweepstakes and contests, and I am not sure what to say in order to win. Would I say the affirmation you used when you were at the casinos on your vacation, or would it be more specific, like 'I request a most benevolent outcome to be picked as a winner for the gift card to Barnes and Noble?'"

———»-o-«———

Lisa, the MBO you gave me as an example for the gift card would definitely work. You could also say, "I request am MBO for winning a prize in this sweepstakes that would be the most benevolent for me, and may it be better than I can hope for or expect, thank you!" This way, you open it up for your guardian angel to get creative. You might limit yourself in some way if you request a specific prize. Keep in mind that the request has to be benevolent for everyone involved.

Alaskan Cruise Bingo

Jeanne writes: "I had decided, after reading your articles a few times in the *Sedona Journal of Emergence!*, to finally check out your website. This was this past July, and we were preparing to go on an Alaskan cruise. I had ordered and received your book but did not have a chance to start reading it before the trip, nor did I remember to even pack it. I was just beginning to get used to requesting MBOs and did them a little sporadically. Anyway, while on our trip, my sister, who loves to play bingo, invited me to join her. Past experiences for me in any bingo games always involved me losing and her invariably winning something. Our first day and game, she won $100. At some point, but I can't remember the exact day, I requested an MBO to win at bingo while on the trip. Well, I went to each game each day. The third day, my husband joined us and in the jackpot game, he won $250.

"The final day came and the jackpot had not been won. The fact that I had not won at all was not surprising to me, but I still enjoyed the game. The jackpot game came, and of course the number of people had multiplied, since the money had to be given away. As I sat there, numbers were being called and none of my cards looked promising. All of a sudden, one card started to gain in the numbers called, and lo and behold, I was down to one number left with about three other people. And then it happened—number seventy-one was called, and that was mine! I won $2,000. Now here comes the most amazing synchronicity to all of this: Upon returning home, I started reading your book. Your chapter on bingo was very similar to my experience on my Alaskan cruise, and the page that this story was printed on was seventy-one—my winning number! I sat and laughed and thanked the angels over and over for all that they'd done. I now request MBOs on a regular basis and know that everything works out for the best.

"Thank you for all the wonderful information you give us. I have forwarded your newsletter to my friends. This wonderful circle of MBOs must be growing very large!" What great synchronicity!"

And as a reminder, as I wrote in the first book, I won half of an $8,400 bingo pot on the last day of my cruise, just as Jeanne did.

RAFFLE TICKETS

Lynn in Oregon writes: "Here is one to share: a crafts fair MBO. My husband and I went to a small crafts fair at the county fairground. It was about one-thirteenth the size of those big city ones, but it was still fun. There were lots of local crafts. We have gone every year since we moved here in 2004. Coming from a big city in Colorado, however, we were a bit disappointed, as we have been with lots of things since moving here. But now we have learned to appreciate the smallness and get over missing the other stuff.

"Anyway, we were at the fair, and there was one section where you could buy raffle tickets to win a prize, something that each vender had donated. We bought four tickets, two each. My husband took his two and looked over things with a quick pass. He said he didn't see anything he wanted, so he gave me the tickets. I was not excited about much either, but the proceeds went to a good cause—maintaining our humble fairground. This was the fourth year, and we had never won anything. But this year, I just wanted to win. I found four things that I wouldn't have minded winning and put a ticket in each one. Before I did, however, I asked for an MBO that I would win one of the things. I was not picky; I just wanted to win!

"That night I got a phone call, and I am sure you know what I am about to say. We won the cutest little locally made birdhouse! My husband makes birdhouses, so he can use this one for a pattern, and then we will put it out with our others. We live on the Oregon Coast and get a huge amount of birds, so this was a good item to win."

LOTTO MBO

Patricia in British Columbia, Canada, writes: "Thank you for the information on birds. I have received your book *The Gentle Way*, and also Robert Shapiro's *Animal Souls Speak*. Both have been extremely helpful.

"When I heard of MBOs from the *Sedona Journal of Emergence!*, I was skeptical at first, but I thought I'd give it a try—nothing to lose, right? Boy was I in for a shock. At first I requested parking as you suggested, and it worked every time.

"Recently I was short on immediate cash and called for an MBO, then forgot about it. I was cleaning out my desk at the time and I came across a yellowed piece of paper with old Lotto winning numbers. I ripped it in two and threw it in the garbage, but then reached down and retrieved it. I asked my son for another form to fill out, as I had already filled one out—he was on his way out the door to go to the store because the draw was in two hours.

"I tore up the first one and replaced it with the other. My son thought I had lost it, since I was using an old ticket. Four hours later when the draw took place, I won $208—exactly the amount I needed. I will never be shy about using MBOs again."

———⟫-◦-⟪———

As I told Patricia, she was the first person to write to me about winning anything on the lottery. I do think it was because this was for a specific need for her as compared to requesting an MBO just to win the lottery.

ANOTHER WINNER!

Anne from Illinois writes: "I've been asking for months for MBOs for winnings at bingo, and finally I revised the way I ask. I asked for my winnings to be beyond my expectations. Yes, I did win a game on the hot ball number. It was the third hot ball jar number and it had a value of $10. Imagine my surprise when I got $300! It seems that no matter what jar number was called, the winner automatically won the first jar in addition, a value of $300. So all the way around, my winnings exceeded my expectations."

CHAPTER FIFTEEN

BENEVOLENT OUTCOMES FOR YOUR PETS

I f you are like most people, you consider your pets to be part of your family. You love them and receive much love in return, and you feel distress when they become ill or lost for even a short time. In this article, I'm going to give you some suggestions that can lower your stress level when events seem to be worrisome or when you find yourself in a crisis situation with these lovable family members.

We found one of our dogs, Sandy, at a local animal shelter, where she was brought after she'd been discovered on the side of a busy highway. A beagle-dachshund mix, she roams the neighborhood if we accidentally leave the gate open, which at the very least could mean the permanent loss of our sweet, lovable dog. Whenever this happens, I immediately say out loud:

Most Benevolent Outcome

"I request a most benevolent outcome for finding Sandy safe and sound. Thank you."

A gentle reminder: Always thank your guardian angel and make these requests with emotion, as that works best.

We always find her, although one time some workmen were holding her in a house they were remodeling down the street from us. When they saw us searching the grounds of the house for the third time (I "felt" that she was nearby), she suddenly appeared. Another time she ran across four lanes of traffic on the busy street we live next to. Most of the time, we find her socializing with other dogs within a one-block radius. Requesting a benevolent outcome always puts me at ease, as I know that I'm going to find her. It takes the stress and worry away.

When it's time to add a pet into your family, you can say:

Most Benevolent Outcome

"I request a most benevolent outcome for finding the perfect pet for our family. Thank you."

If you have definitely decided upon a specific animal—dog, cat, bird and so on—you can be specific in your request, but if you have not decided, let your guardian angel and the universe assist you.

It works in this way: When you go to an animal shelter, one of the attendants there might point out a pet who has just arrived that morning, even just a few minutes before you got there. Or you will be drawn to one particular animal, and in your heart you know that this one is the perfect companion for your family. Or maybe even before you go out searching, one of your friends calls and says her dog or cat has just had a litter of puppies or kittens and asks if you would be interested in coming over to take a look at them. Your guardian angel and guides (or whatever your belief system) work in amazing ways, and I can assure you it's fun to sit back and see how the pieces of the puzzle come together when you make requests for MBOs.

Next you have to choose the right food for your new companion. There are so many foods on the market today that I think it's best to request a benevolent outcome for choosing the right food for your pet. Even your vet can make a mistake in recommending a certain brand or might have a financial interest in his or her recommendation. Let yourself be guided in choosing the right formula and the right amount to feed your pet. And don't forget to request an MBO when choosing vitamins to help keep your pet healthy.

Your pets normally are quite afraid of trips to the veterinarian. I always say:

Most Benevolent Outcome

"I request a most benevolent outcome
for _____ (pet's name)'s visit to the vet."

Our dog Ramsey is so afraid of going to a vet (after being given up twice by other families) that I have to leave his leash off until we are ready to go inside. One of our previous female dogs had a parvo-type disease that is fatal ninety-nine out of a hundred times. We requested a benevolent outcome for her recovery and then had the inspiration to start feeding her large amounts of the same vitamin E we took for our health. Her blood count slowly increased to the point where she completely recovered.

I'm going to give you something else that works when you see an animal on television who has been injured, tortured or trapped. If you love animals (and you wouldn't be reading this if you didn't), you may feel quite frustrated that you can't help that animal in person. But you can do something. You can say out loud:

~~~~~~~~~~~~~~~~~~~~~~~~~~~~~ *Benevolent Prayer* ~~~~~~~~~~~~~~~~~~~~~~~~~~~~~

"I ask that any and all beings come to the aid of this animal, to comfort and assist this animal in any and all ways. Thank you."

These requests are not acted upon by your guardian angel but by other angelic beings, and they are acted upon instantly. Do not limit the request to humans, as it could be other animals or angelic beings who are the ones to actually physically assist that animal in distress. Use the word "ask" instead of "request," as this is a more general phrasing. You will feel better that at least you did what you could to aid that animal. Your confidence will be higher if you have been requesting benevolent outcomes in your life, so you know from direct experience and knowledge that making these requests really works.

Reincarnating as an Animal

Ellen writes: "Do humans, when we reincarnate, always come back as humans? I pray this is so. Could you let me know your answer?"

━━━━◦◦◦◦━━━━

I decided to ask my guardian angel about this in my meditation: Theo, do humans after they have passed on ever return to Earth as animals?

Yes, in some cases, especially in preparation for lives in, say, a jungle area, or in the African wilds. A human will sometimes incarnate or ensoul as an animal to get the lay of the land. It is a preparatory thing souls do to give them a better understanding of their next life. It is usually done by young souls. After you have incarnated a number of times, it is not needed. I will say that your souls easily have this capability, and as we have discussed before, your souls are having millions of lives across the universe at this very instant. Again I reiterate for your readers that your souls are much more powerful and capable than you could ever imagine while you are veiled during your Earth lives—which you volunteered to experience in order to become creators in training. You all have this goal, although it seems you are all quite separate during these lives here.

PET SOUL FRAGMENTS

We previously found out that our pets are fragments of whole souls. Here's another question I just recently asked. Theo, will a dog soul fragment that returns to you bring the knowledge it learned in the last life?

Yes, to a certain extent it does. The knowledge it learned in its previous life with you is buried in its instincts and will show up in this manner. It is not conscious knowledge but is instead deep-seated intuitive knowledge that your dog or other pet will have to draw upon. It will appear that your dog or pet is a fast learner due to this instinctive knowledge.

CHAPTER SIXTEEN

A REMINDER FROM OUR ANIMAL FRIENDS

Patricia from British Columbia writes: "I have been using most benevolent outcomes (MBOs) for about six months now. I have been reading the *Sedona Journal of Emergence!* for years, and I find it most educational and helpful for my entire life. Things have changed so much since I first received the magazine.

"I have osteoporosis in my knees and have a difficult time walking for more than five minutes. Yesterday was a good day, so I went out to the store to do some Christmas shopping. Coming home I decided to stop for a snack. While sitting in the parking lot enjoying my lunch, a crow landed on the hood of my car. It looked at me, we made eye contact, and then it came a little closer. I opened the window and stuck my hand out with a French fry, and it came over, grabbed it and went back to eat it. I again reached out the window with another and it came over and gently took it this time, then it came over and stood on my mirror again. I put my hand out and again, very gently, it took the food, this time holding it in its mouth and not eating it. A second crow came and sat on the car next to me, looking at me but acting very timid. When I looked the first crow in the eye again, it was as though it was telling me this was its mate, so I threw some food out on the ground and they ate and then flew away.

"I was sad that the small birds that I enjoy so much didn't seem to be around the home I recently moved to. One morning while eating my breakfast by the window, I noticed a little bird sitting in the tree right outside my window. I said, 'Good morning,' told it how happy I was to see it and blessed it. Since then, twenty to thirty little birds have come to sit in the tree. Yesterday they were all turned toward me, looking at me. Today we had a big snowstorm and very cold weather, but no birds. I don't know what they were trying to tell me."

⟫·◦·⟪

I think Patricia made a great connection with the crows and the little birds near her house. As we walk our dogs in the morning—or afternoon if it's really cold—I try and say "good life" to any birds we see along the way and whistle. Yesterday one bird was on the ground and hopped away, then flew to the next yard to be even with us, and I whistled. He chirped back. I also wish a good life to any rabbits or squirrels we see along the way. If you read Robert Shapiro's book *Animal Souls Speak*, which I recommend, I think you'll start being more in tune with all the animals that are here to teach us feelings.

RED-BREASTED ROBIN PROOF

Helena in the UK writes: "When I first started doing my MBOs I was trying too hard, and I got fed up with wanting results. One day I was walking through our local park, muttering away to myself, and I said 'I request an MBO for a robin to show me its big fat breast as proof to me that my MBOs are working for me.' I thought to myself, 'Ha ha, this will not work for me,' as I was trying too hard and being quite negative. Well, nothing happened!

"On my way back through the park I requested the MBO again for the Robin to appear. I went on walking, and you will never guess what happened! Out of the bushes shot this robin. It puffed itself up like a fluffy ball and tipped its head to the right as if it was looking at me. I just stood still, as I had full shopping bags in each hand. When this robin appeared, I just got the shock of my life. I just stood there laughing my head off and could not stop. It just happened so quickly, and then it shot back into the bushes. I waited to see if it would come back out, but it didn't. This robin only appeared for about thirty or forty seconds, but it did seem longer. It was just so funny, Tom. I remember every detail like it happened yesterday. Well I most certainly got my proof that my MBOs are working for me. And I most certainly said, 'Thank you, thank you, thank you!'"

MORE ON BIRDS

Patricia's experience with the crows really tickled me. It's a very real blessing to make that kind of connection with a wild animal, especially crows, since they are very intelligent. They are generally taken to be the smartest of all birds—as well as their cousins, the ravens—and I once heard that they are the fourth smartest animal on the planet. I've been feeding them raw hot dogs for years and have had similar experiences, including being followed while riding my bicycle. I'm sure that if Patricia were to go back to the same restaurant, she would have the same experience again with her two new friends. The dollar or two that I spend on hot dogs a week for my flying friends is such a small tithe to enjoy that same gift as Patricia's.

On YouTube search: "Smart Crow," "Smart Crows in Japan" and "Smart little peckers, huh?" I highly recommend watching these videos, as they total only three minutes—well worth your time.

Rabbit Signs

Erika writes: "While I was out for a walk through a green belt near where we live, I realized I hadn't seen any rabbits for a long time. I missed them, as I love seeing them on my walks. There were always lots of rabbits where I go walking, and I wondered if they were killed off or something. So I said an MBO to see one before I got home so I would know they are okay and still around. Then, just before I got home, I spotted one. I felt so happy to see it. Normally they love coming in our backyard each day, but we've had a large dog staying with us for a few months. It felt good to have my MBO happen, as I realized that I had received this as a gift from heaven and that they are really listening, so I said thank you, thank you."

CHAPTER SEVENTEEN
BENEVOLENT PRAYERS

R ecently, I was meditating and I asked Theo how many people who read the metaphysical magazine *Sedona Journal of Emergence!* send white light out to the world on a regular basis. I was appalled to be told that only 10 to 20 percent of the readers actually do this. So I asked my guardian angel to explain: I would like to ask about white light. Few metaphysically oriented people try to send white light, I'm sure because they can't see any results. Can you explain this process more fully to me?

Of course. When you send (or imagine that you are sending) white light out, either over the world or to someone in particular, your guardian angels cover this request, along with a whole group of angels whose job it is to move the light. They act upon your sending of light just like when you send a prayer, and that light is sent wherever you wish it to go. So just think of it as a simple prayer for the world. It is much more powerful than you can imagine, as you as humans are much more powerful than you can imagine. Remember, you are junior creators in training. Sending white light is part of the creation process.

*　　*　　*

Now I'll quickly explain how I send light. You can get creative and send it anyway you wish, but just think what we can accomplish if just a few thousand more readers of this book start sending light every day, or at least on a regular basis. I start by imagining I am sending white light first to North America and Central America; then to South America; on to the Arctic and then to Antarctica; then east to Europe, Africa and the Middle East (sometimes I'll send extra light to specific countries there); then to Scandinavia and eastern Europe; and then to all points to the east. Then I'll switch and concentrate on sending light to all the islands in the Pacific Ocean, the Korean Peninsula, Taiwan, Indonesia, Malaysia, Australia and New Zealand, all of Asia and the Indian subcontinent until the light has encircled the world. All this takes less than a minute of your time. Surely you have a minute per day to give your light to the world!

Apartment Fire

Here's an example of saying a benevolent prayer when your life and/or property may be in danger.

Annette writes: "I must tell you—the other night there was a major fire in an apartment building on the street behind us on the opposite side from us. We could see the black smoke from the kitchen window and suddenly saw huge flames shoot way up. I grabbed *The Gentle Way* and went right to the benevolent prayer on page 98. Eighty firefighters responded and the building was in the middle section of a complex; they had to use three ladders with water cannons. That night on the news we learned that the apartments in that section were empty for renovations, all the surrounding apartments were not damaged and the firewall kept the fire from going to other apartments. All the firefighters were safe and the fire was contained in an amazingly short time. I thanked all the beings who answered this benevolent prayer. I now carry your book with me all the time. Thank you!"

CHAPTER EIGHTEEN

BENEVOLENT OUTCOMES FOR JOBS AND WORK

D iane wrote to me with a really good MBO request that she says: "I wanted to share one MBO that I think everyone else can use, because this is a good one.

Most Benevolent Outcome

"I request a most benevolent outcome for a good, happy, productive, pleasant day at work, thank you!"

"I do this every day and so far have been having some great days at work. I don't get upset, and things fall into place a lot better."

That's an excellent MBO to request Diane. I hope everyone will try it out!

SCREENPLAY BENEVOLENT OUTCOMES

Rick's been working on a screenplay about wrestling.

Here's Rick's MBO story. "I had mentioned before that I paid $1,000 to a producer to read my screenplay and critique it. One of the things he said I needed to do was make the police work more believable, as he was an expert himself. Anyway, I took it to heart. I know an assistant prosecutor in the next county over, but we rarely see each other. I sent an email to the county prosecutor, presented him with my dilemma and told him that I knew Bill from the gym. He replied that I could talk to the assistant prosecutors, but with some restrictions. I requested an MBO for that email and got Bill's email through the forwarding process. I sent him a personal email, but he never replied.

"Anyway, last night, I went food shopping, and to steal from Bruce Springsteen's 'Glory Days,' I was walking in, he was walking out. He said he got that email but wasn't sure it was me. He said he'd be glad to help in any way he could. It took a couple of months, but I guess sometimes we get things when the universe thinks we're ready for them."

ACTING

Joy asked me for an MBO to request for acting work, and this can be used by any actors who read this. I suggested:

Most Benevolent Outcome

"I request a most benevolent outcome for the perfect acting job for me, and may the results be even better than I can hope for or expect, thank you!"

Then stand back and watch your guardian angel work out the details. I also suggested that each time she goes in for an audition she should say:

Most Benevolent Outcome

"I request a most benevolent outcome for this audition, and may the results be even better than I can hope for or expect, thank you!"

Perhaps she's not right for that part, but the producer or director might remember her and casts her in another production. Then she updated me.

Joy writes: "Remember that huge reduction of the hospital bills I wrote you about? Well, the billing department has agreed to let me pay $15 a month toward the $685 and $20 a month toward the $1,500 that I owe. That way I stay out of collections!

"I have also been requesting an MBO around my acting career and have used the phrasing you suggested. Then I asked for a sign that I was focusing on the right direction. I just got a letter from the Screen Actors Guild that they would like me to be on the nominating committee for three areas for Emmy nominations—a total of nine nominations It is a random draw. I got the letter the day after I asked for the sign, pretty amazing, huh? And one of the areas? Best actress in a sitcom, which is exactly what I would like to do.

"Oh, and one more thing—an actor who I met in the fall agreed yesterday to forward my headshot and [resume] to one of his agents to see if I could freelance with this agent for commercial work. I requested a most benevolent outcome about this agent, and may it be better and greater than I hope for!

"I also requested a most benevolent outcome about being on the SAG television nominating committee, and may it be better and greater than I hope for!"

⟫•○•⟪

I think Joy's getting the hang of it.

In the Art World

Steve writes: "So many great things have happened as a result of my using MBOs over the past four years that I cannot begin to express their significance. I have tended to ask for MBOs in relation to pain I feel or discomforting situations. Often I ask that all beings receive the comfort, love or support that they want and need in relation to sadness or pain or fear.

"It is clear to me that the universe has respected my highly sensitive nature by bringing me most benevolent situations so that I may gradually increase my tolerance to interacting with a world that can be frightful for me. I have received jobs, art shows and opportunities for living inexpensively and much, much more as a result of requesting benevolent outcomes."

For Conventions

Laurie writes: "I recently attended a convention in New York and wanted to tell you that MBOs worked for me yet again. A few weeks before I left for the convention, I asked that helpful people be put in my path. Well, were they ever! During my trip to New York, I was asked to submit story ideas for an anthology, was able to put my Atlantis novel directly into the hands of an editor and got a face-to-face appointment with a literary agent. Are my guardians great or what?

"Also, knowing that they were watching my back, I was not as nervous as I otherwise might have been flying for the first time since 2001. I asked for an MBO for a smooth and uncomplicated flight to NYC and they delivered. And I asked the same on the return trip—considering that I was taking off from LaGuardia (we didn't fly over the Hudson). My return flight took off ten minutes early and arrived thirty minutes ahead of schedule. My angels must have wanted me to get home fast, and I did too. I cannot thank you enough for introducing me to the practice of requesting benevolent outcomes. They work every time."

To Increase Tips

Heather writes: "I just wanted to let you know about my most benevolent weekend. I'm a server at IHOP and Sunday was looking pretty slow, so I asked for a most benevolent tip day. Well, by the time I finished with my shift, I'd made $130— just what I'd needed and asked for. Gotta love it!"

I suggest to Heather and to anyone involved in serving the public that you say each time before you begin work:

Most Benevolent Outcome

"I request a most benevolent outcome for tips today, and may they be even better than I hope for or expect, thank you!"

For Calming Yourself

Cindi writes: "Just wanted to let you know about our MBOs at work. I lent a copy of your book to my coworker. We work in a very stressful environment and both of us have started requesting MBOs that everything go smoothly. We do this every day independently. We have had such a good response. Each day we remark how well things turn out. We are always ready to say thank you to our angels and guides, and now I want to say thank you to you too for bringing this gentle way into our lives."

For Finding a Job

Julie writes: "Keep requesting MBOs in your life, and remember to be specific. Ask for exactly what you want. I have been having such great results! I got a gas station job three weeks ago because I asked the angels for an MBO to help me get a job right away, as we really needed the money. Then I asked for a better job, where I could make the same amount or more money, something that would be flexible to allow me more time with the kids and allow us to go to the lake with my parents for their anniversary. There was only two weeks until the trip, and I admit to really not thinking there was enough time, but I kept believing the angels would come through.

"Last week I saw an ad—after not looking in the paper for a couple weeks because I had the gas station job—for an overnight position at a crisis nursery, which is a place where parents can bring their kids for a few hours or days if they have a crisis. A social service position was the direction I wanted to go in. So I sent an email and they called Friday and set me up for an interview yesterday. I asked the angels for an MBO to get the job, and then right before I left for the interview, I asked for an MBO to get the job on the spot so I wouldn't have to go back to the gas station.

"I went to the interview and it went well, but she told me there were two more interviews and the paperwork could take a week or so. By the time I drove home, she had called and had set up the two other interviews and by evening they'd hired me. I start training this week—more money, a job I really want, more flexibility and all in the same day! And we get to go to the lake this weekend. I am totally amazed. Please, if you haven't, do ask for MBOs, and be specific! Do this for everything in your life. I have been communicating with the angels for a long time, but asking in this way really works. Also, is there any benevolent prayer we can say to help with the current economy?"

———————•◦•———————

For the economy I would suggest everyone say this benevolent prayer:

Most Benevolent Outcome

"I ask that any and all beings comfort and assist those who are out of work, and assist in creating employment for all those who wish to work, thank you!"

FOR A SON'S EMPLOYMENT

Arlena writes: "On Wednesday night I requested a benevolent outcome for my son. On Thursday he went to a job interview, and by the time he got home, they'd hired him for the job. Thank you again and again."

⸺⸱◦⸱⸺

Thanks, Arlena. Normally you say a benevolent prayer for someone else, but a benevolent outcome request works if you have a connection with that person, especially if he or she is living with you until the person finds employment.

FOR A NURSE

Christine in Arizona writes: "My cousin Anne (from Illinois) is a friend or acquaintance of yours, I believe. She sends me your newsletter, and also sent me your book on angels. I spoke to her this morning, as I have been looking for a job as a nurse here in Arizona. I was given a referral by a woman I have never met, and it seems to have worked out for the best. The reason I am writing you is because I was reminded by my cousin to request an MBO on my ride there for a safe drive, and then once I arrived to ask for a positive outcome for the interview.

"My cousin also felt that I was there and told me she stopped to pray and request an MBO for me too. It seems as though, after two months of looking for a job, I may have finally found one!"

For Taking Classes

Lyn writes: "I wrote to you back in December about doing some classes and (no surprise here) the most benevolent outcome has occurred. I was a little disappointed that I didn't get approval to teach at the local community center, but I knew that the most benevolent outcome was just around the corner.

A lovely woman who just opened an art studio near me asked me to do a feng shui blessing and then invited me to teach there. We haven't worked out details yet, but it will be in April.

"I have a strong wish and desire to take one of your workshops, so of course that is my current request—that resources become available to do just that! So many wonderful, happy outcomes have been occurring daily. I love the gentle way!"

<hr />

Notice how trusting in MBOs works? Lyn knew that someplace better was going to be made available. You just have to trust that the results will be the most benevolent for you.

For Interconnected Situations

Erika from Australia writes: "I have been reading your articles and the first few chapters of your book, *The Gentle Way*. I found your website, and my hubby Michael and I have enjoyed what you have put on it very much. You may have addressed this question, as I haven't read everything yet; I have ordered the book from a website in the U.K., as there is no charge for shipping."

"I have been doing MBOs since I first read one of your articles, one that appeared last Friday in an Australian magazine. I read the article on the train going to the city, and after I read it, I didn't want to read anything else in the magazine! And I started saying MBOs for my evening of doing angel readings at a city function. I whispered them behind my hand as I sat next to the window. I actually enjoy the readings more than normal now. When I had to work out the money with the hostess, I said an MBO for the amount, as I wasn't too sure what to charge, as things had changed over time. So I said a figure to her and then went to the toilet, saying another MBO. She gave me way more than I'd asked for, which I had thought had been high enough. I went home and said to my hubby, 'Guess what I got paid for the evening for three hours of work?' He was amazed. It was a good feeling and a good first MBO.

"My next MBO was for a Sunday event I was hosting at my home, and I said a general MBO for it. Saturday night the guy running the event rang to say he couldn't make it and suggested we cancel. I ended up agreeing, even though it didn't feel quite right doing it and disappointing the people who'd planned on attending. I sent a message to two friends and told one about an event the next day at a Universal Insights Expo, which I had seen a flyer for a few times over the previous week. Someone I knew who was starting a healing center was going to have a stand there. So I said another MBO for going to this myself and having the best time, and wow, what a time I had! I ran into the two friends who had planned on coming to my event, and instead all of us were at this expo. I had a great time talking with people and seeing all the stands, and there at my friend's stand sat a woman who had been disappointed about my prior event cancellation. It worked out well for her and for all of us. My hubby and I had a good outing and enjoyed ourselves.

"So I learned that requesting a most benevolent outcome can mean that anything can happen, even something that appears bad—but there is a higher plan up there. It took awhile for me to let go and forgive myself for canceling the event even though there was a most benevolent outcome. I have said a whole lot more MBOs, too many to write here. I enjoy saying them.

"I would also like to ask: When requesting MBOs as a couple in a situation together, how do you go about this? Have you any thoughts about this? I know you say them for yourself and I understand they work in this way, but when you are in a restaurant and you say it together for your meal, for instance, how is it best to do this?"

—————»·◦·◄«—————

Erika's question goes back to asking for benevolent prayers when you're requesting something for someone else, although you can request MBOs and there is the radiant effect. Requesting MBOs can be one of several tools you have available to you, although you'll find over time it will become perhaps the major one for coping with the challenges you face in life.

For Computer Repair

Rajul writes: "First of all, thank you for providing the book *The Gentle Way*; I have passed this on to so many of my relatives and friends, and they also use MBOs regularly and are amazed at the miracles taking place.

"Today I would like to inform you about the miracle that took place at my husband's business. He runs a print shop and his work is based on network. One of his computers that does all the graphics would not start and just kept on blinking its lights. He had a computer technician come in and look at it who informed him that the power source had fried and that it needed a new one. Guess what? Before all that had taken place, I had said a living prayer for the computer to be just fine and had also called in Archangel Michael to do the needful work and repair it. After a couple of hours, the computer simply started working on its own. There, isn't that a wonderful miracle? I thank you from the bottom of my heart for introducing me to MBOs and their wonderful gifts. Thank you, Tom!"

OHIO BENEVOLENT OUTCOMES

Peggy writes: "Requesting MBOs has changed our lives here in Ohio. We're having some major construction work done on our home, so I requested an MBO for our carpenters' workday. Before they left that day, they remarked that they didn't know what happened but their work just flowed effortlessly and they got so much done!

"I told my husband Joe about MBOs, and he was so excited about trying them. We both do them every day now throughout the day—it's a wondrous feeling to know we are not alone in this journey. This past Monday, Joe asked for an MBO prior to leaving for an out-of-town workshop he was teaching. His fellow teacher came in to work that day horribly sick, so Joe said he could handle the class all by himself. His co-teacher has sixteen years of experience and Joe is a new teacher with only eight months of experience with weatherization techniques. Eight months ago, he was milking cows at an organic dairy and working at Walmart. Our area is very economically challenged, and it took him two and a half years to find his present job. Everything was on the line for him with this class.

"The class turned out great. His twenty-seven students all wrote great reviews of their experience with him. Also, his new bosses were impressed that he was willing to handle the class by himself and that he did so well. Joe's confidence has soared and his future looks bright with this company and in this new field.

"I do upholstery and continually ask for MBOs on every piece of furniture I work on. I was behind in my orders because of a recent move we made and all the construction work going on around here, but now I'm completely caught up and once again feel professional, on time and excited about the magic of creating beauty. I was assisted in clearing the backlog by my angelic helpers. Thank you, Tom, for sharing this incredible awareness!"

<hr/>

And thank you, Peggy, for sharing some great MBOs!

In Sydney

Judy in Sydney writes: "After reading your article in an Australian magazine, I rushed to order *The Gentle Way*. I eagerly awaited its arrival in the post. I just finished it and wanted to tell you how much it has benefited my life. Although I have always worked with angels, the MBO method is much more concise and effective. I have been practicing MBOs for two weeks now, and they have worked particularly well with little things, such as conversations, events, driving and so on.

"I am waiting for the most important thing in my life right now—to get the best job for me that will cover my expenses. My current job has been cut back to two days per week, and I am not able to pay my mortgage and expenses. The MBO I requested is:

Most Benevolent Outcome

I request a most benevolent outcome for the perfect job for me that will use my talents and abilities and provide more than enough income to cover my expenses.

"Do you have any better suggestions? Also, can you tell me how often I can say the same MBO? I've been saying it several times a day—whenever I start worrying about my situation. I figured it was better to say an MBO than to worry. I also wanted to ask you, is it a good idea to say the same MBO several times a day?"

———

For Judy and all of my new readers, you can say, "I request a most benevolent outcome for the perfect job for me, thank you!" You only have to say this once, as it frees your guardian angel to start working to make that happen. It might be weeks or months, and you might land an interim job because someone else might have the job you requested and will have to leave first (benevolently). Change up the MBOs each day. Request one when you look online for jobs, for finding something in the paper or each time you go for an interview. Also, request an MBO each time you go out to network with friends.

Don't forget to say the "expect great things" mantra. Theo says you will see some amazing things begin to happen when you say that each day.

FOR A DOG NANNY

Lyn writes: "I've had so many great MBOs that I couldn't wait to tell them to you. Our first class based on your book is happening this Saturday. Everything just dropped into place!

"I also have fun news about my living situation, all the outcome of requesting MBOs. I've been a professional dog nanny and house sitter for the past two years, sharing the rent at my daughter's apartment even though I spend very little time there.

"She is off to do some traveling and I thought, wouldn't it be nice to not have rent and utilities? So of course out went the request for an MBO, and I came up with a lovely apartment (for free) in exchange for some dog sitting (which I love).

"Then I was thinking about heading to the country on weekends, and the brother of a friend, who happens to have a stone house on eighty acres, wants someone to live in his house once in a while so that it looks cared for, as he only uses it four times a year and it otherwise sits empty. Oh yeah: for free! Cool, huh? So I now have free housing for my times in between dog nanny jobs—no rent, no utilities!

"I think maybe the most fun thing about requesting MBOs is not worrying about how something is going to come about; it just does, thanks to our guardian angels."

JOBS IN MUSIC

Blake in Hawaii writes: "I answered an ad for a guy looking for a warehouse space in which to store and play his drums. I needed a drummer, and I currently rent a warehouse with a studio apartment attached here in Honolulu. The drummer,

whose name is Kimo, and I met and he moved in. He brought
in an electronic drum set made by Roland, a real basic kit—a toy,
really. We started to jam just for fun. He spoke about how awesome my music was, and that after the first of the year he would
have more time. He volunteered to help me record a demo.

"He came over four times and we played. Christmas came
and he said he would be unavailable until the first of the year.
When I hadn't heard from him, I called on the sixth, but there
was no return call—nothing.

"I was jonesing to play by this point and re-requested the MBO
for a perfect team to back me up with my music. Later that day
an acquaintance introduced me to a music enthusiast he knew
with a Myspace page with over 28,000 friends. She called me
and we talked, at which time I told her about my drummer issue,
and she asked 'Would you like to audition my grandson? He's
looking for a band.' Well, it turns out her grandson is twenty and
has played for fourteen years. I, of course, said yes and called
him, and he asked if he could bring his buddy around to play
bass. We had an instant connection. We have had only four
rehearsals, using the electronic drums left behind by the first
guy—the grandson had a really cheap acoustic drum set, and he
was thrilled to get to play the electronic set. He appears to be
a wizard of some sort when he sits down to play—he loves the
music! And he is only twenty. What an affirmation of the potential of my material.

"During our first rehearsal he said out of the blue 'I don't
think the drummer is coming back for his set. He just gave it
to you." In that moment I felt Kimo make the decision to leave
me the equipment and never come back. He has keys, but he
mentioned that his ears hurt from playing. I am hoping that
something like that is what moved him to stop playing.

"Anyway, we'll be recording in the next week, I'll send you some tracks. I still have not heard from Kimo, but without his drum set, my current band would not have what it would take to do this. How weird of a benevolent outcome is that? All kinds of things seem to go like that for me when I hold the faith that it will all work out.

"Here is one last thing for your readers to consider: I have paid all my bills but have not been able to replace an amplifier that blew up. I play through two amps but have been making one work for rehearsals. I have spent many hours looking online for something I wanted to buy but have received the thought repeatedly that what I want to buy is not on the market yet, though it will be available soon.

"I found the unit yesterday at a music store that doesn't usually sell this unit! I explained to the store manager the solution I needed. He seemed very agitated, but after about two minutes of hemming and hawing, he announced he was going to show me his personal unit even though they didn't sell them. It was available only online, as the company had no dealers in the U.S. Anyway, the unit is being released next week after the NAMM show with what spirit says are the various updates and refinements made since the prototype was released (the manager owned an early unit). Now I know why I didn't have money to buy something that I ultimately would not have liked!"

Wrongful Termination

One of my readers (I won't use his name) emailed about asking what MBOs to request for a wrongful termination lawsuit he was forced to bring against his company. He described his boss as a real jerk who even sexually abused a female employee.

He was concerned that his boss might be fired. I told him this might very well be a soul contract lesson his boss needed to learn in this life, so he should only be concerned with his own actions, as this is probably a soul contract lesson for him too.

I covered this in my first book, for those of you who haven't read it. When you have problems at work, you first ask for an MBO for the problem you're having. You can also request MBOs each time you meet with a supervisor, the managers of a company, union officials, an attorney or even a government agency if what they are doing is against the law. Then anything that happens will be the best for you in the long run.

In the book I related how I was sued for a million dollars one time and the final result was that I paid nothing, except for the attorney fees. Have faith in requesting MBOs for the small all the way up to the major events in your life!

CHAPTER NINETEEN

BENEVOLENT OUTCOMES
WHEN WORKING IN RETAIL

I've been a business owner for over forty years, so I have an overall understanding of working in and operating a business, and I have worked in retail. If you work in a retail store, I believe I can give you some suggestions that will assist you in having less stress and worry in your job.

So let's begin with the start of your day. Whether you travel to work by car, bus, subway or train, you can say:

Most Benevolent Outcome

*"I request a most benevolent outcome for a safe
trip to my store today. Thank you."*

Repeat the request for your return home each evening. If your store is in a high-crime area, request an MBO for your safety during your walk to and from your store and all throughout the day. All of these requests work best when said with emotion. I live in a pretty safe area of my city, but I don't even go to the grocery store without requesting a benevolent outcome for my trip to and from the store, post office and so on.

One of my friends, Josephine, recently drove to a store close to her house to pick up some organic fertilizer. Coming out of the parking lot, her car was hit by a Dallas police car traveling about seventy miles per hour with no lights or siren. The impact knocked off the front end of her Toyota Sequoia. She was not injured, but the police officer suffered a broken knee, and the wreck closed down a busy four-lane street for over four hours. Things can happen, even close to home.

Although these may seem like minor requests, I can assure you that the first time you see a wreck occurring in front of you that you're not involved in or your bus narrowly misses hitting a truck, you'll become a believer about making this a habit each day. You'll know you're being looked after the first time a police officer strolls by as you're locking up the store, just as you notice some unsavory characters standing nearby.

When you walk into your store each day, state:

Most Benevolent Outcome

> "I'm expecting great things today. I am open to abundance and will accept it joyfully!"

Then say:

Most Benevolent Outcome

> "I request a most benevolent outcome for attracting customers and sales today, and may it be even better than I hope or expect. Thank you."

This works whether you are an employee of the store earning the majority of your income from sales commissions or the storeowner. Buyers will seem to appear just as you are done making another sale, and you'll hear comments such as, 'I was just driving by and I suddenly decided to stop in to see what you have.' Your guardian angel arranged this for you, so each time this occurs, be sure to say thank you one or more times.

If you are in charge of hiring, you want the best people, people who are not only best for the open position, but also who are able to work amicably with the other employees. When you are interviewing people, request a benevolent outcome for hiring the perfect person for that position—whether it is for sales, accounting or even a shipping clerk.

If you are the person who is in charge of purchasing goods from vendors, then you can say:

Most Benevolent Outcome

"I request a most benevolent outcome for choosing the most salable goods for my customers and obtaining the best prices, the best quality and the best terms from my vendors. Thank you."

You may find that they unexpectedly offer you better prices and terms, even if you have not asked for them. Or they might suddenly offer an item that you had not thought of before, which becomes a best-seller for you.

As a business owner, there are times when you must find financing for your store to make it grow or to pay off short-term debts. You may need bank financing or investors. When you meet with a banker, say:

Most Benevolent Outcome

"I request a most benevolent outcome for obtaining the financing I need at the best rates. Thank you."

If you don't receive it from that bank, it's because another bank or way of financing will be made available to you that will be even better. Trust the process. It works perfectly.

What are some other requests for benevolent outcomes you can make?

- Request an MBO that your store and goods remain safe and secure from shoplifting.
- Request an MBO when you meet with your accountant at tax time.
- Request an MBO when you must utilize the services of an attorney.
- Request an MBO when a customer asks you for advice about which items to purchase.
- Request an MBO if you are looking for a better location for your store.

Online Retail

Diana writes: "I have used MBO requests every day for the past two months. The one time I forgot to use them was the day things did not flow smoothly and spiritually in my life.

"I have used MBOs to find missing items and to get taxis, and used compression of time to get to appointments on time and to finish scheduled tasks. I also used MBOs to ask for help with our new Internet server. We noticed that the day we switched to a new server, orders dropped for our online business. My partner was a bit worried and stressed out about it, and I immediately requested an MBO for business to pick up, and that the technicians would find and fix whatever problem there was with our new server. The result was almost immediate. It was a relief to know that MBO requests can help with technical and technology issues.

"I have recommended your book and website to anyone willing to listen, and most importantly, I've told them about these awesome prayers. I hope I can help more people by spreading the news."

⟫-◇-⟪

In my office we've had to request MBOs several times in the past few months for technical problems with our computers. We've been able to overcome these problems each time by requesting MBOs.

CHAPTER TWENTY

EXPECT GREAT THINGS

The first thing I do every day is to say out loud: "I'm expecting great things today, great things tomorrow and great things all this week, thank you." I have noticed that people will suddenly contact me to buy something, or people that I had really given up hope of doing business with again contact me to complete a deal. In my active meditation, I asked Theo about this: Theo, please explain how saying the phrase "expect great things" assists us, if at all.

Yes. This phrase does open the door, Tom, and acts benevolently to clear the way for good things to happen. It does act like a benevolent request, but in a slightly different way. It is similar to the benevolent outcome request "and may the results be better than I can hope for or expect." Your guardian angels will cause events to happen that you would never know to request. Yes, it does push aside the deep-seated restrictions many people have about allowing good things to come to them. This phrase should be said every day if possible. You will be amazed at the good things that occur in your lives after you say this a few times.

After mentioning this in my weekly newsletter, **David in St. Louis wrote:** "I have just had a great week. I started saying this prayer every day since Monday morning, and the following things have happened: My wife has been trying to sell a client's building for almost a year with problem upon problem—from evictions, to stolen condenser units (twice!), to city inspection issues, to finding a buyer but then dealing with all sorts of loan problems over multiple lenders. This client/deal was taking up 90 percent of my wife's time. At the same time, the owner was very negative and fearful of his situation, and in my opinion this exacerbated the problem and kept things on the same course for a long time. Well, after starting this new prayer, which is quite open-ended, a strange thing happened. This client made an intention to be more positive, and lo and behold, the building sale was completely finished by Thursday of that same week. It's amazing that through using this prayer I helped myself, my wife, her client and everyone who had a vested interest in this deal. And another thing: I received a bonus from my company. It was expected, but in my mind the time frame was unknown. This occurred on Friday. My week has been just incredible!"

FOR A WRITER

Laurie writes: "I'm so glad you mention the great things mantra (as I now call it). I've been saying it since you mentioned it, and have reaped some wonderful results. One example: I'm a writer, and work is tough to get. Not long after I began verbalizing the great things mantra each morning, an editor called me up and invited me to submit a few story ideas for a science-fiction anthology he is putting together. Believe me, I'm going to be asking for MBOs on that too. I'm also quite convinced that the combination of MBOs and the great things mantra are working to help me find the perfect agent and for selling my novel about Atlantis. Already two agents have responded to my query letter and have asked to see the first three chapters."

WHEN IN NEED

Jan writes: "I was sick this winter and out of work. I requested a most benevolent outcome (MBO) for assistance on everything. I even asked an MBO for people to plow my driveway, for I could not afford the plowman. Four or five different men noticed my driveway needed plowing over the winter and plowed it for free. A high school friend of mine (whom I have not seen or spoken to in a few years) happened to be doing a job nearby, and he plowed quite a few times. A neighbor who lives down the road that I don't even know very well plowed for me as well.

"My children (fifteen and eighteen) and many of my friends now use MBOs; they have seen the amazing results that I have had using them. I recently heard a spot in which Michael Jackson told a reporter that he asked for a really good song to come to him, one with a great beat. A few days later, he said, he was driving down Ventura Boulevard and the beat of 'Thriller' came to him."

And I would like to mention again that each morning I say:

Most Benevolent Outcome

"I expect great things today, great things tomorrow and great things all the rest of this week, thank you!

My guardian angel tells me in my meditations that this acts very similar to a benevolent outcome request and can really make a difference in your life after starting to say it each day.

Right after Michael Jackson's unexpected death, one of my producers called me and said he was going to do a quick documentary on the pop star, as he already had several hours of footage and was filming more interviews and buying more footage. Since then I have sold this documentary to several countries at good prices, with good commissions, and more sales are on the way. This was quite benevolent for my company in an extremely slow period for business. This was truly something that I could not have anticipated or requested an MBO for.

I AM AGELESS

August 26 is my birthday, and this past year it was okay as birthdays go. Something I haven't mentioned before: When someone asks me how old I am, I always say, "I'm ageless." I say that for a psychological reason and a metaphysical one. I think that virtually everyone has a concept of what someone is "supposed" to look and act like at age twenty, thirty, forty, fifty, sixty, seventy and eighty years. By saying you're ageless, you remove that concept from your subconscious mind.

The metaphysical reason I say this is that I believe that someday scientists will prove that our cells are cognizant and actually communicate with each other. I believe you slow down the aging process by telling your cells that you are ageless. If you get in the habit of doing this, as I have done over the years, it will be really difficult at times to remember your age when you need to fill out some form. You'll have to count up from your birth date. Think about this and perhaps make it your own habit.

Kelly writes: "I couldn't resist telling you this. I have been using the affirmation you suggested recently stating about being ageless. You mentioned how you sometimes had to do the math to figure out your age since you began using the affirmation regularly. Well, the other day I stated my age to an acquaintance but didn't realize until today that I was wrong! I had stated last year's age. My birthday is in August, so I'd had practically four months to get used to that number—but no!

"In fact, as I reflected on the number I told her, I realized that I don't even feel that age. It's like the number, or any number in general, is just an arbitrary label. I just didn't relate to any specific number as being my age, and I still don't. I wonder if this has to do with the affirmation, and I suspect it does. In years past, when asked my age, I'd state the number coming up, like that age was already looming on the horizon. I find this encouraging, this reverting to youthfulness, so to speak. Thanks for your suggestion!"

TIME COMPRESSION REVIEW

Both in the first book and in the *Sedona Journal of Emergence!* I've discussed how we can manipulate time to a certain extent. Here is an example: If you're running late for an appointment at 2:00 PM and it's already 1:30 PM, and it takes forty minutes to get there, you can say, "I request a compression of time until 2:00 PM, thank you!" Then don't look at your watch or clock. Typically, you'll arrive a couple of minutes early.

Kelly writes: "I wanted to share a compression of time request incident I experienced yesterday morning. I was headed to work and noticed that I was running a bit later than usual, as there was road construction at every possible route I could have taken. I decided to request a compression of time and decided on the specific time when I would arrive at work to be by 8:07 AM. That essentially meant I'd make it to my office by 8:10 AM with twenty minutes to prepare for the day—thus the seemingly strange time I chose, in case you were wondering.

"Well, I intentionally avoided looking at the clock, noticed a last-minute switch of route that seemed right and took it. I arrived at the building I work in, but for some reason, I turned into the wrong parking lot. I hadn't parked in that one in two or three years. Why I turned in there, I couldn't imagine. Then I looked at the clock and realized why. It was 8:06 AM, and the time it took me to pull out of that lot and go around the building to my usual lot was precisely the time it took for my clock to read 8:07 AM sharp! I chuckled aloud as I realized specifics are honored! I could have stated 'by 8:07 AM or earlier.' Maybe next time!"

CHAPTER TWENTY-ONE

ACTIVE MEDITATIONS

T he Reverend Pat Robertson announced on his television program "The 700 Club" on January 2 that there would be a "massive terrorist attack" that would possibly kill "millions of people," and that there would be "major cities injured." I found that interesting, so I thought I'd better check it out. I asked the question during my active meditation. Here is what I received from my guardian angel, Theo:

Could you talk a bit about Reverend Robertson's prediction of a massive terrorist attack?

The Reverend Robertson is mistaken in his prediction. This will not be allowed to happen again in this country, as the lesson has been taught. This is simply a way on his part to gain national publicity for himself and his program. He attracts what he fears, so his imagination tells him that there will be a huge event when there will only be a small one, as we have discussed before. The terrorist influence is waning, although you cannot see this yet. It will certainly go unabated in the Middle East, and specifically in Iraq, but there will be very little terrorism in the rest of the free world. I think that is specific enough for you at this time.

After reading this several times, I thought I should ask for more on what lesson we were being taught, so a couple of days later I asked the following question: What lesson it is that we have learned?

When you meddle in other countries' affairs, there can be a severe backlash that will affect your country and all of its residents. Instead of taking a militaristic action, you could have continued to negotiate and bring other parties—other countries—into the negotiations with you. Instead, your president listened to his military advisors and invaded a country. Now you are paying with the lives of your military men and women, those who are killed and wounded. Also, you will have a very heavy financial burden that, as I said before, will take generations to pay off: The huge cost incurred in the invasion. The only way to peace on Earth is through diplomacy and negotiations—talking—and if needed, sanctions against the offending country. But face-to-face talks always work the best, as those countries can hear your country and other countries' concerns and respond accordingly—even if dictators run said country.

I thought initially that the major part of my contract in this life was to help introduce requesting benevolent outcomes and benevolent prayers to the broader public. I decided to ask Theo about explaining my active meditations: Is part of my contract or purpose to get more people to meditate, or will that just be a by-product of the process?

You are supposed to significantly aid in assisting people to meditate—whether it is starting to meditate or helping them to meditate in the active way. It's something that was left for you to discover, as we cannot tell you everything. Then there would be no fun in the dis-

covery, you see. As you tell people how easy it is to get started, there will eventually be a flood of people who will at least try to meditate. This will help them to raise the vibrational level of not only their own beings, but of the world in general. So yes, keep plugging away in mentioning this to people.

❋   ❋   ❋

I guess you will continue to hear me talk about meditation for the foreseeable future. Really, if I can do this, anyone can. You just have to start and keep at it. During the months since I began meditating (in July 2005), I was disappointed in my progress in becoming more accurate at receiving these thought-packet messages, as Theo calls them. I kept asking how my accuracy was doing, and I was repeatedly told, "practice, practice, practice," so many times that I finally stopped asking. It's like any skill. Some people can pick up a skill immediately, and then there are those of us who have to really work at it. You must make a commitment to it, just as I encourage you to make a habit of requesting benevolent outcomes on a daily basis.

I only have time to meditate at most four times a week with my busy schedule. I also found it difficult at times, after I'd been doing it for some time, to come up with new questions for Theo. I keep a spiral notebook at my desk to write down questions between meditations. Sometimes it's time to meditate and I have no questions on the page. Then I will go back over previous meditations and find subjects to delve into more deeply. And then there are times when I can't write the questions fast enough. Guess who's helping me!

FOOTBALL TEAM LOSS

Here's an example of a rather mundane question I asked, although any sports fan will understand this one, especially if their team has just lost an important game. We watched one of the weirdest American football games I have ever seen, between Dallas and Seattle: I watched a football game last night, and we rooted for the home team and even said benevolent prayers for them, but through bizarre plays, they lost. Was that supposed to happen for some reason?

You are correct in your suspicion that there was more afoot, to use a pun, in the results of this game. There will be personnel movements—people moving to new jobs, losing their jobs and so forth—that are designed to happen for the growth of those individuals and their life contracts. When you have that many people on each team—including the players, the coaches and even the administrative personnel—then there are certain events that are preordained, if you will, that must happen in order for all of these people to have learning experiences and challenges with regard to the sports life they've chosen to experience in this incarnation. These are all very complicated occurrences.

Now I can report that two years later that was exactly what happened. The head coach resigned, several coaches went to other teams and a new head coach was hired, and he hired coaches and scouts and so on.

ADAM AND EVE

Doesn't everyone want to know about Adam and Eve? Who seeded the Adam man and woman on Atlantis and elsewhere?

It was a combination of off-world cultures that look very much like yours, Tom, but they each contributed DNA to the experiment so that your bodies would be hardy enough to survive being veiled and having to make your own way with no prior knowledge allowed to assist you. Each life was and always has been seemingly your first and only one, so that only we guardian angels, as you call us, were allowed to interfere or assist you in any way.

How many years have people had blue eyes. Some people say it is around 7,000 years.

Much, much longer than that, Tom. People have had this color of eyes for perhaps a million years. The genetic code was introduced that far back in time for you. I think you suspected that, but I am confirming that suspicion. Your records just do not go back any further than that, so that's why that number is used. It has nothing to do with fact.

THE ILLUMINATI

Recently, we went to a press screening of *Angels and Demons*. I recommend seeing it on DVD or television if you haven't already. After watching it, I asked Theo about the Illuminati. Theo, is there still a secret society known as the Illuminati, and if so, do they have any influence in the business or political world?

Yes and yes, Tom. This secret society is also known as the Sinister Secret Government, and they do have great control over some large banks and corporations, and certainly in the political arena as well. They keep themselves quite hidden, but there is a council of these people that exists. They are extremely powerful, but their power is slowly diminishing, and as you get closer to the transfer to the fifth dimension, their power will continue to diminish. They have tried to slow this down, but it's like standing in front of a locomotive that is moving slowly down a track—it's impossible to stop. More will come out about these people in the months and years to come, as they will be unable to stay completely hidden much longer.

✳   ✳   ✳

Quite some time ago I spoke with Gaia, the soul of the Earth:

Gaia, will those people who make up the Sinister Secret Government, the Illuminati or the cabal go through the shift too?

That is a question that has not been decided yet. Probably they will not, which of course is a major reason for their concern. They are steeped deeply in third-degree machinations and they will not find life so enjoyable when things are so much more amicable after the shift. As you may have guessed, these souls are not ancient like your own, but are younger in the sense that they still have much to learn about life on Earth and how to live peacefully with each other.

THE AKASHIC RECORDS

Theo, when a person is regressed under hypnosis to remember a past life, are they tapping into their akashic record or are they able to tap into memories held at a higher level or what?

Tom, they do tap into their akashic records to view a past life. That is why I've said before that the akashic records are available for anyone to view. When a person is regressed, they are told to go to the life most affecting the present life, so they automatically—with a little help mind you—find the akashic record that records the particular life most pertinent to the soul's present life. It's not so hard—it's just not done very frequently, even by those that have undergone a regression. You are not meant to live in the past but only in the present. When the past negatively affects your present, then it is good to access a particular record to find the cause, and then there is a release, as there is a sudden understanding of why present life is being affected.

AN EXTRATERRESTRIAL IN COLORADO

I recently watched Larry King's television show [in June 2008] and he mentioned an extraterrestrial sighting. Was the Gray that appeared at the window in Colorado in 2003 real?

Oh yes, it was, Tom. This was a young Zeta who wanted to see for itself how earthlings live and got caught as a peeping Tom, although it was decided by those higher up that this would be good. It was a chance to keep the idea of extraterrestrials in the public view, since at a point not too long into our future, they must make themselves known. The year 2015 is not too far off, you know, and there will be an increase in sightings and such leading up to that ten-year period when the extraterrestrial civilizations will make themselves known. It will be quite exciting, as you can imagine.

Elvis Presley

Theo, Elvis Presley made a huge impact on the music world during and even after his life. What can you tell me about this soul fragment and what his next incarnation will be?

Yes, Mr. Presley was quite charismatic. He has had other musical lives in the past, as that is his soul's emphasis: music in all forms. His next incarnation, which he already is having, is in the past—he'll be an opera singer this time around. As you are not too familiar with opera singers of the past, you would not recognize his name. He will have more lives both as a singer and as a musician. He will be famous in some lives and not at all in others. And there will be balancing lives, just as there are for everyone.

The Future

According to Bashar, as channeled by Darryl Anka, between 2015 and 2025 we will know for sure of the existence of other extraterrestrial civilizations. Is that energy still in place, and if so, how will that come about?

Yes, they will begin making themselves known, as you will be at a higher level of vibration and spirituality, having learned secrets kept from you for hundreds and even thousands of years. It will make it that much easier for governments to finally acknowledge that they have been in contact with these civilizations for many years.

Naturally, as you've read and heard, the process will be a gentle one with petite, non-threatening, humanoid peoples being the first to contact you. Certainly this will cause a sensation even under those parameters, but the beings who will come forward will have had much experience in these matters with first contacts on other worlds, so they will make their existence known in the most gentle way possible, so as not to frighten too many people.

Will this happen in the United States first?

No, not necessarily. It may very well be in Europe.

SUICIDE

Theo, explain suicides for me. Why do they happen? Is it part of a soul contract?

Yes, suicides are a difficult subject. As you can imagine, there are innumerable reasons why they happen. It can sometimes be souls very new to Earth who are just overwhelmed with life here—they took on too much for such an early life, so they opt out, so to speak. They take their own life because of the stress of their Earth lives. As you can imagine, this causes them to incur karma that must be balanced in a future life, as they must eventually suffer what their loved ones suffered when they took their own life. And they must be the ones also to comfort loved ones in a future life that have had the same loss when another loved one passes.

All aspects of a suicide must be balanced. Then there are the times when souls volunteer to take their own life through drug over-

dose and such in order to give that experience to the families and loved ones and friends of that soul as a teaching experience. So you see, there are many, many reasons why a suicide can occur. It is an experience that the soul must have during one or more lifetimes in order to understand and learn and gain knowledge for the future. I've already explained to you before that a soul will have lives where it acts as the "bad guy"—someone who rapes, kills, steals, cheats and so on. Again, every soul who starts to have Earth lives must eventually experience every conceivable life there is with all human passions.

THE SOUL FRAGMENT HITLER

Theo, tell me about the soul fragment that was Hitler. Most people, depending upon their beliefs, would think his soul was wiped out. But he did incarnate to be the main bad guy, didn't he?

Quite so, Tom. He knew that a massive war would give many karmic opportunities to be the bad guys and good guys. But again, as so often happens, he went too far, so like you and others in centuries before, he is now balancing that life with many, many other lives.

How many lives will it take to balance?

Certainly almost a hundred. His soul in the future will be a great leader who will touch everyone in a benevolent manner.

So that life is in the future and not the past?

Yes, that particular one will be in the future.

And I assume that will be the same for all those henchmen of his?

Yes, even more so in a couple of cases.

How many lives had he lived at that point?

Good question, Tom. He was a fairly seasoned soul. He was in the five hundreds. So he understood the enormity of the role he would play, but again he did not stick to his soul contract and allowed others to influence his decisions.

Strange as it may seem to you and others, he did take on the role of the main bad guy out of his love for humanity as a whole, as he knew there would be a great shift as a result, and if you look back at not only what happened in that time period but what came after regarding the respecting of human lives, then much was accomplished in that war to drive people to want peace.

❀   ❀   ❀

As you can see, you can ask questions about anything that interests you. You'll know that you're on the right track when the answers come back completely different than what you thought they would be. Try out active meditation. In the next chapter you will read questions that my readers emailed in to me for Theo to answer, along with Theo's responses.

CHAPTER TWENTY-TWO

QUESTIONS FROM READERS FOR MY GUARDIAN ANGEL

I receive many questions from all over the world that I then ask my guardian angel, Theo, during my active meditations. This is something anyone can do, and Theo tells me that in the future almost everyone will meditate. He also told me to encourage you to do so too. Please enjoy the wide range of subjects covered below.

SOCIOPATHS

Gail in Seattle writes: "I have a question for Theo, if that is okay. I am a psychotherapist and encounter patients who have endured sociopaths (psychopaths) in their lives. Sociopaths are people completely without conscience who are unable to appreciate or create emotional ties to other human beings. I have worked in mental health centers where this is not considered a mental health problem—it can't be fixed. They have actually sent some to local shamans for soul retrieval. Why are there people like this? When they get power, even a little, they cause a lot of pain and destruction for the rest of us. Were they created this way? Do they have souls? Their existence kind of shakes up my belief in people as basically good. Thanks, Tom."

———❖———

Theo, what purpose do sociopaths serve in our lives and what is their soul learning from these lives?

Yes, a good question from your reader. They do have a purpose. It is to remind everyone that you do have feelings and how bereft life is without these feelings. Sociopaths are born with a flaw in their DNA, which will eventually be discovered (and will then be able to be fixed), so the age of the sociopaths, if you wish to call it that, will soon come to an end. Again, this is done for the benefit of teaching everyone about lack of feelings, but also for the doctors and researchers who will one day find a way to correct this DNA flaw. Sociopaths' souls gain the knowledge of what lives are like without feeling any remorse for their actions—how there is an absence of love in their lives. It has been a very useful teaching tool for these souls who could never experience that in any other life in the universe.

RACE CONFLICTS AND FOOD SHORTAGES

Diane in Maryland asks: "Will we ever have the race conflict in this country that was once predicted, where we would have a war within our country of different races killing each other off? Does Theo see a future world where we suffer with water and food shortages here in this country?"

———❖———

Theo, will there be any more race conflicts in the United States?

No, you are finished with those now, thanks to Mr. Obama. You reached a higher level than expected, as we have noted before. Yes, there are still a large number of racists in the United States, but their numbers will continue to dwindle as they see that those of other races are just as capable and in many cases more capable than they in working at high levels of intelligence.

Will the world suffer food and water shortages in the next few years?

Yes and no. Certainly parts of the world will suffer food and water shortages, but it will never become a worldwide event with all suffering. More nutritious ways of feeding the population will be discovered and implemented. Humans are quite resourceful, as you're quite aware. You will find solutions for all these problems. After all, you are the solution finders of the universe, and that's another reason you will be so successful when you go to the stars and to planets and societies that have become stagnant in their growth. You will find solutions for them, born over millions of years of finding solutions yourselves while cloaked with no knowledge of your true grand selves.

THE CHRISTIAN BIBLE

Theo, the old texts that were considered for inclusion in the Christian Bible—do they all still exist? It was reported there were 130.

Yes, almost all still exist, and as you guessed, most will be found in the Vatican Archives, with only a few located elsewhere that were considered too radical for the church to keep. They were some of the first texts, yes, but there were others from other cultures, so they have a treasure trove of history that will be released one day soon for study by scholars–not just biblical scholars but also by archeologists who wish to locate certain ruins described in these texts. It will be an exciting time for historians and for the public as these old texts are released for study.

Theo, Marie wants to know whether the Bible was written as metaphor or as literal truth?

It was written by men but was changed drastically, as we have previously discussed, in A.D. 327. These were simple people who passed stories down, and then those stories were changed to serve the purposes of greedy men who wished power and riches.

Marie wrote back to me, Theo, asking what we are to believe, if the Bible is written by men?

Certainly this is a philosophical question, Tom. A fairly short answer would be to be led by your heart and your intuition as your own guardian angel attempts to assist you with every minute of the day. Listen to those whispers in your ear, as they will guide you. If you read something that doesn't feel right to you, then reject it and continue with your studies elsewhere.

As I have said before, the Bible was corrupted by those who wished power and money. One day much of the Bible will be rewritten, as the Vatican archives will be opened and missing passages will be restored, along with missing books that were rejected back in A.D. 327. It will take quite a few years for this to be accomplished, as the passages and books will be revealed in stages, but it will happen, I assure you. Until that time, listen to your own guardian angel, who wants only the best for you.

[Theo refers here to the Council of Nicaea, if you wish to do your own additional research.]

THE ENERGY OF SNOW

David from St. Louis writes: "Can you ask Theo to explain something about how the geometry of snow affects us, especially as it's falling? Over the years I've noticed a strong sense of peace and a heavy spiritual feeling when snow is falling, especially when conditions allow for large flakes to fall. I suspect that it's something about the higher intelligence present in the geometrical patterns in snow. Can you find out more?"

Theo, is there some energy in falling snow that gives us a sense of peace and tranquillity?

Yes, snow crystals have an energy about them that radiates peace. More studies should be done on these crystals and measurements of this energy should be taken. It will surprise your scientists. Eventually their instruments will be sensitive enough to take even better readings and there will be more of an understanding of what snow does—the calmness and peaceful energy it radiates.

UFO Over Washington, DC

Marie writes: "I have a question. I watched the inauguration on television. I went online and on CNN, and they captured a UFO by a monument near the White House. Is there a reason why that happened? What can Theo tell us?"

——•◦•——

Theo, Marie says a television camera captured a UFO over the Washington monument during the inauguration. Your comments, please?

Yes, there was some activity around the DC area, as there was a tremendous amount of benevolent energy being broadcast from the enormous assemblage of people who came to see the inauguration. They were taking measurements that are beyond your understanding on a 3D level, but yes, they were there, and yes, something was captured on television for an instant or so during the event. This event lifted vibrations around the world, Tom. As I have told you before, Barack Obama will be a great peacemaker, not only in the United States, but around the world. He will have a great legacy.

Barack Obama's Lineage

Renee writes: "I understand from other sources that Barack Obama is the reincarnation of Abraham Lincoln. But I have also read that Al Gore was too. How can this be? And if true, are they fragmented souls of Lincoln? And also how interesting that they are both in the same political era at present time."

Theo, Renee wants to know if Barack Obama is the reincarnation of Abraham Lincoln.

Yes, he is. I know you are surprised by that answer, but Mr. Lincoln—his soul—wanted to finish the job he started and truly bring peace, not only to the United States, but to the world in general. This time he will be more successful.

Theo, is Al Gore also the reincarnation of Abraham Lincoln?

No, he is not. He does a soul lineage that connects him to other famous people in history, but he is not the reincarnation of Lincoln.

Anyone I would recognize?

Yes, but more in ancient times. Caesar Augustus was one. This time he is, shall we say, balancing the scales to help increase people's awareness of the fragility of the Earth, and he has accomplished much to help start Americans in particular caring and starting green-Earth plans.

REQUESTING MBOs FOR ILLEGAL ACTIONS

Pauline writes: "I recently purchased your book after being introduced to MBOs by a friend. I have used them successfully for small things and am building my confidence in my angels (and myself) to work on bigger things. In reading the book, I ran across a section that raises a huge question in my mind. It pertains to illegal aliens and in particular the word illegal. Is it reasonable to expect our angels to give us an MBO when we are knowingly doing something that is against the law? I understand completely that sometimes one feels backed into a corner and have no choice, but does that then mean if a person is hungry and decides to break and enter a house or rob a business that he/she should request an MBO for the deed?

"I am having great difficult believing that angels would protect someone who chooses an illegal activity that deliberately harms another. Of course, that also means, I believe, that crossing the border illegally harms the citizens of this country because this causes a huge tax burden on tax-paying citizens, increases the crime rate and so on. Thanks. I love your book (except for the part in question) and the concept of asking for MBOs."

<hr />

One of the rules for requesting benevolent outcomes is that it must be benevolent for not only yourself, but for all those involved in the request, even if you request something that is not benevolent either in error or on purpose.

A person who crosses a border illegally is following his or her soul path. These people may be caught and sent back, they may be preyed upon by bandits and rapists, they may die of thirst or freeze to death or they may be successful in their attempt. That is not for you or I to judge.

Also, our soul paths are affected too. Do we show them compassion or treat them as the scum of the Earth? There are lessons for the population of this country too. Perhaps we all will have to see the other side by having a life as an illegal alien. All lives must balance eventually. So please send illegal aliens love and light. As Tenzin Gyatso, the fouteenth Dalai Lama, said, "If you want others to be happy, practice compassion. If you want to be happy, practice compassion."

In the first book I also have a section with an MBO for prostitutes and other people who work in the night, that they remain safe by requesting a benevolent outcome. Do I condone prostitution? Of course not, but the vast majority of prostitutes are victimized, so I tried to give them hope, if they ever read my book.

Pauline emailed back and asked: "Thank you for your reply, Tom. I am still stuck on the word 'illegal,' and unfortunately, your answer does not give me the clarity I was hoping for. My question was not about my judging their illegal activity, but about whether the person breaking the law could or should ask for an MBO for that activity. In other words, if I decided to cheat on my income tax return, would it be appropriate for me to ask for protection from my angels for deliberately cheating? I will ask for an MBO regarding resolution of my own conflict with this issue."

So I asked Theo: Someone wants to know what the results would be if you asked for an MBO for cheating on your income taxes.

A deep philosophical question, Tom. Yes, I sent you a picture of a great shark or fish devouring you. It really depends what a person's soul contract is. What are they trying to learn this time around? If you do not pay your fair share of money to your government, then perhaps you will be caught, or perhaps not. There are lessons to be learned either way, so there is no one answer. If you are hoarding the money, there will come a time when that energy flies out the window. If you use that money for others' welfare instead of lining the pockets of some government bureaucrat, then that is a learning experience too. Again there are no right answers, only lessons to be learned.

I assume you would have a similar response if someone requested an MBO to steal.

Yes and no. Yes, there are learning lessons, but when you steal from others, you incur karma, and that has to be balanced in this life or a future one, when you will have things stolen from you and will feel the same anger and heartache someone else felt when you violated their space–their house, home or business. That must be balanced.

Soul Experiences

Renee from Lake Tahoe writes: "I have been following your weekly conversations with Antura (a being living in the Sirius star system on a water planet) with much interest and I have some questions for you. I know that we all have origins on different planets and have chosen to come here to planet Earth to live many veiled lifetimes. I would like to know what planet you came from and if it was the same as your Sirian friend? I'm aware that I'm originally from Arcturus and that some of my friends are too, but I know some are from the Pleiades also. Is it possible to have some members of your soul family or group originate from different planets?"

⋙─◦─⋘

As a side note, Theo has said that I had many lives on a water planet in the Sirius star system before my lives here. Theo, do members of the same soul cluster or group have lives on more than one planet between Earth incarnations?

Quite so, Tom. It all depends upon what needs to be learned and how these Earth lessons can be used to assist other planets. So you are not limited to one planet, although you may be attracted to return to a planet where you've had many lives before you started your Earth incarnations. But your primary mission is to use the knowledge you gain from your Earth lives and put it to good use elsewhere. Even if that life on another planet lasts a thousand or more Earth years, when you next incarnate on Earth you might incarnate only one day, one week or one month after your last life on Earth, or as we have discussed previously, you might even incarnate in an earlier time period, if there is something that can be learned there, or if your talents can be used in that earlier time period.

Does a soul cluster, or group, generally come from all of you having lives on the same planet prior to your Earth lives?

Not necessarily, but generally yes. Again, the soul cluster could have had many lives on a variety of planets in order to prepare for the beginning of the lives to be experienced on Earth. Remember that spiritual mastery must have been attained before the first Earth life.

Does that include each fragment, just the soul cluster or just the soul as a whole?

The soul, as you know, is having hundreds of thousands of lives across the universe, so spiritual mastery is something attained through these lives. The soul cluster that the soul sends to live on Earth will have attained this itself, and therefore the soul cluster will have that knowledge and experience through the soul, but not necessarily each fragment. A bit complicated, but the soul is aware at all times of all the lives it has chosen to live on many thousands of worlds. Keep in mind the soul's goal, along with all the other souls taking part in the Earth experiment: to take over for the Creator when this Creator moves on to the next level. That's why we have said many times that you are junior creators in training, as you will be one day when you join hands, metaphorically speaking, to become a Creator.

QUESTION ABOUT OUR CREATOR

Diane writes: "Our Creator is very unique among the billions of creators. Is it true that there are several creators and not just one, as we believe here on Earth?"

⸺⸺◈⸺⸺

Theo, are there many Creators, or just one?

Yes, there are billions and billions of other Creators, many making their own universes or exploring what they want to explore. One Creator I've been in contact with is Zoosh, who has taken on the job of keeping the history of this universe, as he was attracted to our Creator's work because it was so unique. Out of the billions of other Creators, I understand that only one other one has gone on to a higher focus level—whatever that is—and our Creator will do that when we junior creators in training join together and take over.

Theo, have other souls joined together in the past in another creation or creations to take over for a creator as our souls (as I understand) plan to do in the future?

No, this will be the first time ever that this will be done. There have been other creators who in the past have taken over a universe for another creator when that creator wished to create something else, but there has never been a group of souls that banded together as you will do. Most of the billions of souls just would not have the capacity to handle the billions of decisions that your creator handles each moment.

You can read the history of this universe in Robert Shapiro's *Explorer Race* series. It's the best I've ever read.

REIKI BANNED BY CATHOLIC CHURCH

Shannon writes: "I am a Reiki Master and am teaching Reiki and trying to spread the word about this wonderful healing energy. It has made quite an impact on my life. I was just sent an article from the Reiki magazine with the following information: 'Recently a committee of Catholic bishops wrote a statement saying that Reiki is based on superstition and Catholics shouldn't use it. More specifically, they said it shouldn't be used in Catholic hospitals or healthcare centers, or by Catholic chaplains.'

Is Reiki a healing energy that is helping our advancement or just another thing we've made up? Being from a Catholic background, I do not have any trust in the Catholic church, but it saddens me they are saying this."

Theo, is Reiki a valid healing modality? Why would the Catholic Church try to ban it?

Yes, of course it is a valid form of healing. The Catholic church wants to ban it for several reasons. The first reason is out of ignorance. They don't understand how it works. The second reason is that, because they don't understand it, they are fearful that it could be some form of Satanism, which—as you and others know—it is not.

So as it always happens, ignorance breeds fear and their actions spring from that fear. It will take some time for them to accept Reiki as a form of healing, and yes, they like to think they possess the only form of spiritual healing. But there are many forms of healing, and more will be discovered in the coming years. Their congregations will have less and less of a need for their services.

Torture and Abuse of Animals

Please explain the torture and abuse of animals. What part of a contract does that play?

Again, this pertains to a life where the soul must act as a bad person. The animal souls who volunteered to be part of the teaching process of souls having human lives understand that this must happen. It not only teaches the soul about animal abuse, but it also teaches other souls to have pity, revulsion, sympathy and so on, which are necessary traits to learn during the human experience. Those who show great empathy for the plight of these animals do help to raise the vibrational rate of all humans, and the souls that volunteer to be the bad guys doing these horrible things know that they also must balance these actions out with future lives where they aid and assist animal victims. Everything must balance out, Tom–everything.

Any suggestions for alleviating these problems?

No, actually. You humans are raising your vibration and this will become less and less of a problem for you in the coming years. Those individuals who are inclined to do this now will not be able to make the jump to the next level, as their souls are too new to Earth and will need more seasoning, shall we say—they will need to have more lives in a third-dimensional reality before they can make the shift.

VAMPIRES

Theo, someone wrote and asked if there are any vampires on this timeline or any of the others.

Yes, certainly there are those humans who drink the blood of others. This was a common practice in wars at an earlier time. But you humans have great imaginations, so the story evolved into the creation of vampire stories. There are no such creatures in any timelines now that must live in the dark and cannot come out in the daytime. There are those who have convinced themselves they are vampires, but they are delusional, to say the least.

DEMENTIA AND ALZHEIMER'S

Theo, a lady asked me: if someone requested a heavy pain medication for a relative with Dementia or Alzheimer's that would cause death, would it be considered assisted suicide, and what karma would result?

A complicated question, and perhaps a little difficult to explain. If a person knows that the pain medication requested would cause death, then yes, he or she is assisting in another person dying. But keep in mind that it could be a soul contract for this person to perform or make this request. It could have been all decided that when the soul is put in that position, at a certain point this request for the pain medication be made. If it is a soul contract, then there is no karma involved. This is or would be the case normally. If the person just wished to rid him or herself of the responsibility and did not make the request out of love, then there would be karma that would have to be balanced in another life, or in a few cases in the same life. So you see there can be many answers to the same set of circumstances.

I see. My reader also asks in the same regard, are we required to live our lives to the determined time of transition, no matter the situation involved?

Please remember to remind this person and all your readers that you do have specific soul contracts that require you to experience all passions, all pain and every experience that a person can have during or by the time you have finished all your Earth lives. We have already discussed suicides, and that this could be a soul contract in itself, so what would appear on the surface as an act of desperation might very well be the soul contract for that particular life.

As I have said before, life is much more complicated than it seems on the surface. And it is tremendously more complex on the other side of the veil–way beyond the understanding that you can have in your current dimension.

Tamar writes: "You wrote about assisted suicide for someone with Alzheimer's, which brings up some questions on my part. After the Terri Schiavo case came to a head in 2005 [a husband wanted to let his brain-dead wife be taken off of life support, and her parents sued to keep her alive], I told my kids and husband that if I should ever be in such a situation, I wanted to be taken off of life support. I even prepared a legal medical release to this effect. I went so far as to tell my son that if I ever succumbed to Alzheimer's, I would want him to give me pills so that I could pass on since we do not have a cure for Alzheimer's at this time. This request was made for me as well as for my family so that they wouldn't have to suffer. Now I'm wondering what kind of karma this could incur on them and on me."

Theo, if we instruct our families to take us off life support and/or to give us pills to pass on if we have dementia or Alzheimer's, is there any karma involved in this?

Not really, as this was a choice long before the event. You do have choices you are allowed to make in each life, and if you choose to pass on in this manner, it really doesn't need to be balanced in another life in the same way.

MYANMAR/BURMA CYCLONE

Kerrie from Australia writes: "Referring to the cyclone in Burma/Myanmar in May 2008 and the attitude of the military junta to refuse aid, I must ask why? Only a small amount of aid trickles through, and then the military interferes. There are dead bodies in the rice paddies, diseases and death. How can the Burmese government officials sleep at night? What is their problem? The people have not committed a crime against the military; they are just victims of a fierce cyclone—what gives?"

I asked Theo: What perspective can you provide my readers regarding the cyclone in Myanmar and the ruling military?

Let's see if you can get this, Tom. There are many factors at work here. There are those who have life paths to experience and survive a cataclysmic event as we have spoken about before. There are those whose soul contracts call for them to be drowned. Regarding the military rulers, these are younger souls, yes, who still have much to learn. These lives are earning them much karma that they must balance out in future lives. Of course, part of their soul contracts cause them to act in this manner, so that the souls that chose a life in Burma or Myanmar could experience what they are supposed to experience. Again, things are much more complicated than they appear on the surface. Much is being learned by not only the rulers but also by the people they rule, and by the aid workers and diplomats and everyone connected with this situation. So yes, say a benevolent prayer for these people and for the rulers too. Those prayers, as I have stated before, are answered.

Go Out and Help Someone

I think the following answer by Theo gives insight on several different levels.

Theo, a fifty-nine-year-old lady wants to retreat into a more singular life. Can you provide any insights?

Yes. Because of past lives and karma, she has a deep-seated urge to return to a life as a monk where she was alone and in deep blissful meditation most of the day. That was that life and this is this life, and she certainly has that choice, but it would not be the best life path–the one of most accomplishment and gain. She still has much to learn about people. She should volunteer to help others and she will gain much insight and compassion for those who are having a much harder time in this life. Again, she can choose to sit on the sidelines, or she can be out there actively helping others. It's her choice. Wish her good life for me, Tom, and tell her that her guardian angel loves her dearly. All she has to do is ask for assistance, as her guardian angel cannot assist her unless she requests it.

So you see, you always do have a choice, but there are paths that reward you with much more achievement than others. Just begin by asking for assistance: request benevolent outcomes.

SIDE SOULS, SOUL ENERGY, MAGNETICS

If you're on myspace, post a bulletin suggesting that your friends read my blog, which are reposts of my weekly newsletter. I'm Tom3344. I received the following inquiries through myspace:

Theo, are there such entities as "side souls"?

No. This refers to what could be considered guides. Sometimes people, especially those who allow drugs or alcohol to rule their lives, attract entities that are lower vibrationally and that then attach themselves to these people. Then, as we have discussed before, the "cosmic cops" (as Mr. Dick Sutphen calls them) must be called in to rid a person of these attachments. But for all intents and purposes there are no twin souls as such. However, everyone does have their main guides present to assist their guardian angel throughout your life on Earth.

How much energy does a soul have—and I will say a whole soul, as compared to a fragment like I am?

Tremendous energy, Tom. Your machines that measure energy would not only peak but would break, as the normal soul is extremely powerful with tremendous amounts of energy. Now the person who asked that question was really referring to a soul fragment having a life on Earth. You do have energy, but certainly it is tiny in comparison to your complete soul. More sensitive machines are being developed that will one day accurately measure the energy of the average human being.

What sort of energy machines do other societies have?

That answer would take too long, so let's look at one or two. Most of these societies use a form of magnetics (to keep this as simple as possible for your readers). These machines create great energy, as your society will discover in the near future. Tesla was the first, and as more researchers recognize this, more magnetic machines will be developed that will have hundreds of uses.

Astrology and Numerology

Theo, I was asked about what you think of astrology, astrologers, horoscopes and numerology.

Each of these systems provide glimpses into your immortal personality, Tom. They give you hints as to who you really are, and these horoscopes and numerology readings can give you a small window into your future. So all of this serves the purpose of assisting you during your lives on Earth.

SANTA BARBARA FIRES

Steve writes: "Thank you for your recent reply to my question on the Santa Barbara wildfires. This is an update and follow-up to my previous question.

"After I wrote to you, the situation looked very, very serious for Santa Barbara, and also for Montecito to the south and Goleta to the north, as the fires continued to spread. The next evening the firefighters were bracing for the worst as the sundowner winds were predicted to be gusting again. These winds come up in the evening and blow down the foothills fanning the flames out of control and toward the residential areas. I followed an impulse to request an MBO that the sundowner winds be calmed. The previous day—when all hell broke loose—the temperature in Santa Barbara was a record 101 degrees in the city and much higher in the foothills.

"The next day a marine layer brought cool, damp air in from the ocean. The temperature dropped 30 degrees and the sundowner winds never materialized as predicted by the National Weather Service. Every day I kept requesting that the sundowner winds be calmed. The marine layer remained for three days with no sundowners. For the next three days, the National Weather Service predicted a return of the sundowners, but they never materialized, allowing the firefighters to achieve 80 percent containment and begin scaling down the operation.

"As I write now, fourteen days after the fire first broke out, there is 100 percent containment of the fire and firefighters are mopping up as the fire burns itself out. The city has returned to normal. What a miraculous turnaround to a potentially disastrous situation. I am wondering whether my MBOs and my guardian angel could have produced such a profound effect. Naturally, I would like to think it is possible but find it difficult to believe.

"Would you ask Theo or Gaia if my MBOs and my guardian angel played a major role in this miraculous turnaround or was it just one of many other factors or was it just coincidence?"

———◦———

Theo, did Steve's request for a most benevolent outcome regarding the Santa Barbara fires have any effect, or was it just one of many factors or a coincidence?

Yes, Tom, his request of the benevolent outcomes did have some effect, along with the prayers of countless people in that area. Prayers are answered, as you teach. They don't have to be said a particular way, although what you have shown people in how to say them works perhaps the best, because it is so easy to remember—as compared to trying to make up a completely new prayer each time for something specific for you, especially one for other people and beings such as animals. So to answer Steve's question: yes, his voice was heard along with others, and Gaia changed the weather for them. You are junior creators in training and you must be able to see your successes, yes?

Yes, Theo, of course I agree. We would give up if we saw nothing happening.

Concern About "Any and All Beings"

Starr writes: "I enjoy your newsletter, but I have an issue with your benevolent Prayer. It says: 'I ask that any and all beings . . .' Doesn't that leave things open to non-benevolent beings to step in? Shouldn't it be changed to something like 'all beings from the light . . .'?

"This may be my issue, but would you go out into the street and ask 'any and all people' you meet into your home or mind? I am surprised that someone hasn't put this out there before. Blessings."

I do thank Starr for bringing this up. I find that when I receive a question like this, there are many other people that have this same question but haven't asked.

Theo, Starr has a problem with "any and all beings," as she is concerned that this will attract non-benevolent beings. Your comments?

Yes, it might seem that way on the surface to Starr, Tom, but when angelic beings, as you call them, are called upon to provide assistance, they certainly would not "dial up" shall we say, a non-benevolent being to assist the person that said the benevolent prayer—or for whom they said the prayer for.

These are, as we have discussed before, whole souls Tom, and even though they have not achieved a golden lightbeing level, they still are whole souls and capable of millions of decisions per minute in your time. Please trust these souls to handle any request in a most benevolent way, as they have only the best intentions for the person or beings in the request. It is all accomplished from within the light, so there is no danger of attracting non-benevolent beings.

TOO MUCH OF A GOOD THING?

A number of people have written to me in the past couple of months asking about requesting the same benevolent outcome multiple times. My standard answer has been, as I was told, that you only have to request it one time. Still, the emails kept coming, so I knew it was time to get the answer directly from my own guardian angel, Theo.

Theo, here's a question I've been asked several times recently. Should people only request a benevolent outcome once, or can they request the same one numerous times?

A good question for today, Tom. Yes, if they feel a need to, they can request an MBO more than once, although it is not needed. One request works just as well as numerous requests. We, meaning what you call guardian angels, understand that since you are veiled, you question everything—even the validity of requesting MBOs—and even when you have great success in requesting them. The veil is very thick but it is thinning, and as you have told your readers, requesting MBOs thins the veil and raisers their vibrational level. So if they feel more comfortable in requesting a benevolent outcome more than once, then it is okay, and it will not dilute the request.

*   *   *

So, in regard to Theo's response, request the same MBO as many times as you wish if it makes you feel more comfortable. Your guardian angel will not penalize you if you do.

IN CONCLUSION

E ven as I came to the end of putting this book together, I was still receiving stories and questions, each one better than the previous. Finally I had to cut the book off and submit what you have just read to my publisher. However, the story continues, and if you wish to read all the stories and questions that have been emailed to me since then, go to my website: www.TheGentleWayBook.com. Click on the "Articles and News" link, and start your reading with the newsletter dated June 20, 2009. Then you can read all the archived newsletters up to the present time.

Do sign up to receive my free weekly newsletters, each one different from the previous one. You'll also read excerpts from my next book, in which I ask Theo all the questions you might want to ask your guardian angel about: these great golden light-beings, your guides, timelines, Atlantis, the Land of Mu and much, much more. Also through my website, you can print out a variety of signs to help you remember to request benevolent outcomes each day. Click on the "Signs" link to find my benevolent prayer (the one I say each morning), my "expecting great things" mantra and more. I wish you all a most benevolent and successful life!

DAILY REMINDERS

Even though requesting Benevolent Outcomes is the most simple but powerful spiritual tool you can use the rest of your life, you still have to remember to make using them a habit or, with our busy lives, you'll forget. So if you'll go to my website, www.TheGentleWayBook.com, I have several signs to assist you in remembering. The first sign is:

> ## *Daily Reminder*
> *Request most benevolent outcomes today!*

Just click on "SIGNS" and you'll find this sign that you can print out and attach to your bathroom wall, the refrigerator or even in your car!

Another great sign that you'll find there is:

> ## *Daily Reminder*
> *"I expect great things today, great things tomorrow and great things all the rest of this week, thank you!*

If you'll start saying this every day, soon you'll be seeing pleasant surprises during the week that were totally unexpected. And each morning I say the following benevolent prayer you can also find under SIGNS:

Daily Reminder

"I ask that any and all beings assist and comfort anyone that I have ever harmed either physically, mentally, morally, spiritually or emotionally in any past, present or future life, and I ask any and all beings to assist and comfort the families and friends of anyone I have ever harmed in any way, in any past, present or future life, thank you!"

Theo says that saying this Benevolent Prayer each day will do more than you can possibly imagine to balance your lives. These signs are a great resource, so be sure to use them!

APPENDIX B:

RECORDING DREAMS

As I mentioned at the beginning of this appendix section, these are bonus points, things that you don't have to do to successfully request benevolent outcomes but that can really enrich your life.

I have been recording my dreams each morning since 1979—a long time! I have recorded thousands of dreams. Many times I can't recall any dreams, and the most dreams I have ever recorded in one night were nine. There are many books on dreams, so this will just be a short introduction to them.

Why record your dreams? Because most of the time they are messages from your guardian angel. I have had many precognitive dreams. One time many years ago, my wife and I were going to attend a world congress of travel agents in Manila. I had a very vivid dream of an explosion, and somehow a woman and several men were involved. Based on that dream, we cancelled our time in Manila and added extra days in Taiwan and Hong Kong. The first day of the congress, a bomb exploded at the front of the hall, injuring ten people. A woman who worked for the Philippine government in Los Angeles in some capacity and four men were arrested. That happened early on in my dream recording, so you can imagine how seriously I took it from that time onward!

During the time when my wife and I were selling our wholesale tour business, I was looking around for what I would do next. I had a vivid dream about "four-walling," which was a practice that independent filmmakers of family adventure films used in the 1970s. They would go into a town or city and rent a theater for one or several nights and advertise in newspapers, on the radio and perhaps on TV. They kept all the revenue from the box office, and the theater kept the concession stand sales. I couldn't understand why I had that dream, but before long I went into international motion picture and TV program distribution.

Most of the time, dreams are symbolic in nature. Before a Delta Airlines plane crashed at the Dallas-Fort Worth airport in August of 1985, I dreamed of a Delta-shaped aircraft crashing. Before the 1986 Challenger shuttle exploded during the launch, I dreamed of being in a glass capsule high above the Earth and then being under the ocean. I had three precognitive dreams before 9/11, including one where I saw a tornado going across the face of a building with a group of people floating in the air right behind it.

I use a dream dictionary to assist me in interpreting dreams. You may not need one—several of my friends and family do not—but if you do, I suggest going to your local bookstore with several dreams written down. Look those dreams up in several dream dictionaries to see which seems to be closest in interpreting your dreams, and buy that one. The book I have used for years and years is The Dreamer's Dictionary by Lady Stern Robinson and Tom Corbett.

To record your dreams, do the following:
1. Purchase a spiral binder, a pen with a bold point (to see in the dark) and a small pen or reading light.
2. Place them next to your bed on your nightstand.
3. Each night, record the next day's date and the town or city where you are recording the dream.
4. Say out loud, "I wish to remember my dreams tonight."
5. Buy a dream dictionary if you have a problem interpreting your dreams.
6. After a period of time of recording your dreams, you may wish to do what I do, and that is to print special binders with a hundred sheets printed front and back at a local printing place. You can go to my website, www.thegentle-waybook.com, and copy and paste the page I have already created. I like this size, as it fits on my nightstand more easily than a full spiral binder especially with a dream dictionary, other books and magazines, your small light and a lamp already on there.

I have heard countless times over the years, "Oh, but I don't dream." That is absolutely not true. Everyone dreams. But if you don't demand that your conscious mind remembers your dreams, then they are lost immediately upon waking. Again, there are books on dreams and how to remember them, but here are a couple of suggestions:
1. Say out loud each night that you wish to remember your dreams.
2. Tell yourself to awaken five or ten minutes before your alarm goes off.
3. Try to awaken as quietly as possible. Do not turn on the radio or the TV.
4. If you awaken during the night, think about what you have

been dreaming and immediately record it. You will probably not remember the dream in the morning.

5. If the dream seems to be a warning dream, say:

Most Benevolent Outcome

"*I request a most benevolent outcome that if this
dream [or dreams] affects my personal life, I will have
a benevolent outcome. Thank you.*"

Good luck and good life!

APPENDIX C:

MEDITATION

Another great thing for you to try, if for no other reason than your physical health, is meditation. I have been in my doctor's office one hour after meditation, and my blood pressure count was so low that they had to retake it twice. I have done a quick version of the breathing exercise I describe below just before and during a blood pressure test/ heart rate test, and have seen a drop from eighty heartbeats to sixty-six in just thirty seconds or so!

Many, many doctors recommend meditation these days. A study conducted in the fall of 2005 found that the brains of people who meditate were 5 percent thicker in the areas that deal with focus and memory than those of nonmeditators. The implication is that meditation may actually improve attention span and memory [*U.S. News and World Report*, December 26, 2005].

But meditation offers you so much more. If you have a problem in your life—and who doesn't?—you can ask your guardian angel for the solution. You just have to quiet your mind and listen for the answer.

As you progress in feeling more comfortable in your meditations, you may wish to ask all sorts of other questions about people you know and those in the news. As an example, I saw an interview on TV with Paul McCartney, and he said that he didn't actually hear John Lennon or George Harrison say change this or that, but he implied that he felt their presence and assistance. So I asked in meditation what their connection with him might be, and I was told that they are now acting as guides for him and assist him in writing music. They also assist him in making other musical decisions as well.

Recently I bought the Bob Dylan documentary DVD, No Direction Home. I had heard his music many times over the years, but when I watched the documentary, I was impressed with the many different types of songs he composed, so I asked in a meditation about that. The message I received was that he still does not understand the "process" and thinks he just made it all up in his mind, but there were actually a number of different cosmic songwriters who contributed songs. I saw an image of a line of songwriters standing there and someone saying, "Next." Many of those songs helped make people think about their relations with other people.

So to begin the practice of meditation, follow these easy steps:

1. Try and choose the same time each day to meditate. This might mean you set your alarm twenty minutes earlier each morning—and yes, you may have to change your sleep time to adjust to this. Or perhaps at work after lunch, instead of watching TV or rushing off to have lunch at a restaurant, you can close the door to an office or even go into a closet.

2. Have a notebook handy where you can write down what you receive, as the messages are similar to dreams in that they will fade away quickly (I switched from a notebook to my computer due to the length of the messages).

3. I suggest that you play some nice soft music to cut down on outside noises. You may have to put headphones on

to listen. I listen to music by Robert Coxon, a Canadian artist who plays some really beautiful music.

4. Sit comfortably in a chair, on a sofa or on the floor. Sit in an upright position—don't slump. Ask for a benevolent outcome for your meditation.

5. Close your eyes. Put the tips of both thumbs and forefingers together.

6. Begin breathing in through your nose, holding to a count of four, and then gently blowing out through your mouth, with your lips just barely open. This helps center your attention. After a little time, continue to breathe in through your nose and out your mouth without holding the breath.

7. At the same time, relax your body, allowing your muscles to relax from the bottom of your feet slowly up through your legs, your torso, your arms, your hands and your neck. Most importantly, relax those mouth muscles.

8. Start purposefully to quiet your mind. Push any thoughts of your many daily activities gently away. This is the hardest part. It will take you some practice, because your mind will want to jump around to a hundred different subjects.

9. As you quiet your mind, imagine a beautiful white light filled with pure love coming from your guardian angel down through the top of your head. This will help you focus. Let this beautiful loving light from your angel travel slowly through your whole body—first down through your head, then to your throat, then through your heart and solar plexus, then through your stomach, past your groin area and on down through your feet. Imagine it going through the floor all the way to the center of the Earth.

10. Now imagine a golden light going out from your heart and surrounding your whole body in a spiral motion like a

cocoon. Then expand the light and imagine it going all the way around the world. All of this is helping you focus and visualize.

11. Now, while still gently breathing in through your nose and out through your mouth, imagine yourself walking down a set of stairs. The stairs have numbers on them. Go from seven all the way down to one. As you walk down the stairs, think, "Seven, down, down, down, six, down, down, down," and so on. If you feel the need, go down another set of seven stairs.

12. At this point, you can keep your mind quiet and imagine yourself in some beautiful quiet place like a beach or a mountain. See if there are messages or images that come to your mind. Or if you have a question, gently ask it in your mind and then wait for the answer. Don't jump to another subject or let any other thoughts distract you. It will seem as if you are thinking the answer, but you're not.

13. When you feel it is time to come back, imagine to yourself that you are walking back up the stairs, and as you count from one to seven, you will be fully awake. Record any feelings, images and messages that you received.

Don't become frustrated if your first few attempts do not seem to have results. This is like riding a bike. It takes a little practice, but do you remember how much fun it was to ride that bike successfully? This is even better!

There are books on meditation if you wish to take it further and learn more about it. If you want to buy a meditation CD, you can go to www.dicksutphen.com. In my opinion, Dick has one of the best voices I have ever heard. Choose one of his several guided meditation CDs for a most benevolent outcome for your meditations!

WARM HEART MEDITATION

This is a meditation whose purpose is to acquaint you with the feeling of physically and mentally loving yourself. After I give you the directions for this seemingly simple exercise, I will describe the many benefits that can result from doing this.

Close your eyes. Take your thumb and rub it very gently across your fingertips for about one minute while doing nothing else. Notice that it focuses your attention on your physical body and away from all the other things around you.

Next, bring that same physical attention toward your heart or anywhere in that area where you can look for or generate a warm feeling. This might not be your heart; it could be your solar plexus or abdomen. It may take a minute or two to find or generate warmth that you can feel.

Go into that warmth, and stay with it and feel it for a few minutes so that you can memorize this method and so your body can create a memory of how it feels and how it needs to feel for you. At different times, it might be in different places. Don't try and move it; just feel it. As you continue to repeat this exercise, you will be able to do it for longer periods of time.

Afterward, think about this: *The warmth is the physical evidence of loving yourself.* You have read for years about how we need to love ourselves, but most of these have been mental concepts. This is a physical experience of loving yourself. It unites you with your angels and all of creation. It will provide you with a greater ease and comfort in life.

You may notice as you get better at this that your friends and acquaintances will be more relaxed around you and that things seem to be more harmonious. You will tend to not become upset as much as you used to. Animals may react differently to you—they will be more friendly and relaxed around you, perhaps look at you differently. This is because you are radiating out this warm love energy.

Do not try and send this to other people. If they are interested in what you are doing or why they feel better around you, you can teach them this simple meditation. Again, this will benefit you and improve your experience along the Gentle Way.

GLOSSARY:

ANGELS: Divine intermediaries who assist in arranging benevolent outcomes and living prayers.

ANGEL SPEAK: Words such as "benevolent" and "living prayer" that seem to be used in the angelic world.

BENEVOLENT (BE-NEV-O-LENT): A kindly disposition to promote happiness and prosperity through good works, or by generosity in and pleasure of doing good works [definition from Webster's Dictionary].

GUARDIAN ANGEL: An angel who volunteers to watch over a particular person throughout his or her life.

GUIDES: Angelic entities who assist a guardian angel in giving guidance to an individual. These can include deceased parents, relatives or friends.

HIGHER SELF: Your soul.

HOPE: Desire accompanied by the expectation of obtaining what is desired or belief that it is obtainable. [definition from Webster's Dictionary].

BENEVOLENT PRAYER: A request made to your guardian angel and other angelic beings when it is for others. This may include you as well.

MBO: Abbreviation for "most benevolent outcome."

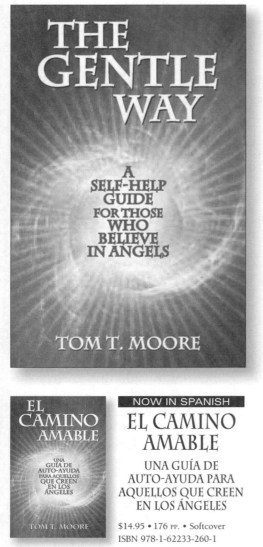

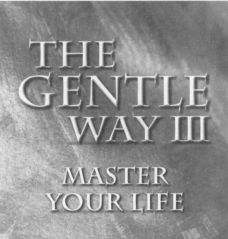

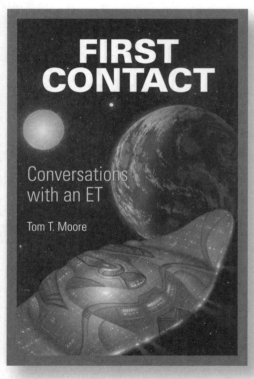

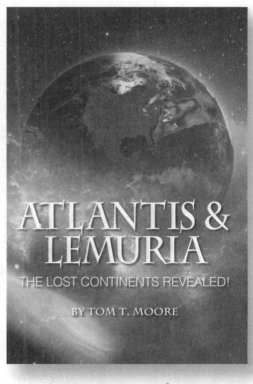

278 ✦ **Light Technology** PUBLISHING *Presents*

TO ORDER PRINT BOOKS
Visit LightTechnology.com, Call 928-526-1345 or 1-800-450-0985,
or Check Amazon.com or Your Favorite Bookstore

THROUGH DRUNVALO MELCHIZEDEK

THE ANCIENT SECRET OF THE FLOWER OF LIFE, VOLUME 1

Once, all life in the universe knew the Flower of Life as the creation pattern, the geometrical design leading us into and out of physical existence. Then from a very high state of consciousness, we fell into darkness, the secret hidden for thousands of years, encoded in the cells of all life.

Now we are rising from the darkness, and a new dawn is streaming through the windows of perception. This book is one of those windows. Drunvalo Melchizedek presents in text and graphics the Flower of Life workshop, illuminating the mysteries of how we came to be.

Sacred geometry is the form beneath our being and points to a divine order in our reality. We can follow that order from the invisible atom to the infinite stars, finding ourselves at each step. The information here is one path, but between the lines and drawings lie the feminine gems of intuitive understanding.

$25.00 • Softcover • 240 PP.
ISBN 978-1-891824-17-3

You may see them sparkle around some of these provocative ideas:
- remembering our ancient past
- the secret of the Flower unfolds
- the darker side of our present/past
- the geometries of the human body
- the significance of shape and structure

Drunvalo Melchizedek's life experience reads like an encyclopedia of breakthroughs in human endeavor. He studied physics and art at the University of California, Berkeley, but he feels that his most important education came after college. In the past twenty-five years, he has studied with over seventy teachers from all belief systems and religious understandings. For some time now, he has been bringing his vision to the world through the Flower of Life program and the Mer-Ka-Ba meditation. This teaching encompasses every area of human understanding, explores the development of humankind from ancient civilizations to the present time, and offers clarity regarding the world's state of consciousness and what is needed for a smooth and easy transition into the twenty-first century.

🕯️ *Light Technology* PUBLISHING *Presents*   279

TO ORDER PRINT BOOKS
Visit LightTechnology.com, Call 928-526-1345 or 1-800-450-0985,
or Check Amazon.com or Your Favorite Bookstore

THROUGH DRUNVALO MELCHIZEDEK

THE ANCIENT SECRET OF THE FLOWER OF LIFE, VOLUME 2

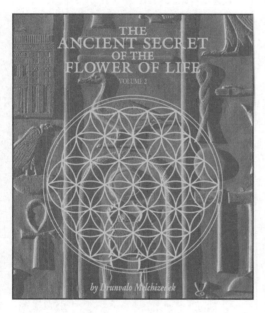

The sacred Flower of Life pattern, the primary geometric generator of all physical form, is explored in even more depth in this volume, the second half of the famed Flower of Life workshop. The proportions of the human body; the nuances of human consciousness; the sizes and distances of the stars, planets, and moons; and even the creations of humankind are all shown to reflect their origins in this beautiful and divine image. Through an intricate and detailed geometrical mapping, Drunvalo Melchizedek shows how the seemingly simple design of the Flower of Life contains the genesis of our entire third-dimensional existence.

From the pyramids and mysteries of Egypt to the new race of Indigo children, Drunvalo presents the sacred geometries of the reality and the subtle energies that shape our world. We are led through a divinely inspired labyrinth of science and stories, logic and coincidence, on a path of remembering where we come from and the wonder and magic of who we are.

Finally, for the first time in print, Drunvalo shares the instructions for the Mer-Ka-Ba meditation, step-by-step techniques for the re-creation of the energy field of the evolved human, which is the key to ascension and the next dimensional world. If done from love, this ancient process of breathing prana opens up for us a world of tantalizing possibility in this dimension, from protective powers to the healing of oneself, others, and even the planet.

Topics Include
- The Unfolding of the Third Informational System
- Whispers from Our Ancient Heritage
- Unveiling the Mer-Ka-Ba Meditation
- Using Your Mer-Ka-Ba
- Connecting to the Levels of Self
- Two Cosmic Experiments
- What We May Expect in the Forthcoming Dimensional Shift

$25.00 • Softcover • 272 PP.
ISBN 978-1-891824-21-0

BY DRUNVALO MELCHIZEDEK

LIVING IN THE HEART

Includes a CD with Heart Meditation

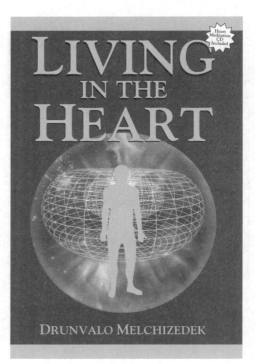

"Long ago we humans used a form of communication and sensing that did not involve the brain in any way; rather, it came from a sacred place within our hearts. What good would it do to find this place again in a world where the greatest religion is science and the logic of the mind? Don't I know this world where emotions and feelings are second-class citizens? Yes, I do. But my teachers have asked me to remind you who you really are. You are more than a human being — much more. Within your heart is a place, a sacred place, where the world can literally be remade through conscious cocreation. If you give me permission, I will show you what has been shown to me."

— Drunvalo Melchizedek

$25.00 • Softcover • 144 PP.
ISBN 978-1-891824-43-2

Chapters Include
- Beginning with the Mind
- Seeing in the Darkness
- Learning from Indigenous Tribes
- The Sacred Space of the Heart
- The Unity of Heaven and Earth
- Leaving the Mind and Entering the Heart
- The Sacred Space of the Heart Meditation
- The Mer-Ka-Ba and the Sacred Space of the Heart
- Conscious Cocreation from the Heart Connected to the Mind

TO ORDER PRINT BOOKS
Visit LightTechnology.com, Call 928-526-1345 or 1-800-450-0985,
or Check Amazon.com or Your Favorite Bookstore

SHAMANIC SECRETS SERIES
THROUGH ROBERT SHAPIRO

Shamanic Secrets: Lost Wisdom Regained

Due to wars, natural disasters, a shaman not being able to train a successor, and many other reasons, Isis (through Robert) says that 95 percent of the accumulated shamanic wisdom has been lost. Now it is important to regain this wisdom as young people who are able to learn and use these processes are being born now.

Beings who lived as shamans and healers on Earth at various times now speak through Robert Shapiro and bring these lost teachings and techniques to a humanity waking up and discovering it has the talents and abilities to use this wisdom for the benefit of all.

$16.95 • Softcover • 352 pp. • ISBN 978-1-62233-049-2

Shamanic Secrets for Material Mastery
Explore the heart and soul connection between humans and Mother Earth. Through that intimacy, miracles of healing and expanded awareness can flourish.
$19.95 • Softcover • 528 pp.
978-1-891824-12-8

Shamanic Secrets for Physical Mastery
The purpose of this book is to explain the sacred nature of the physical body and some of the magnificent gifts it offers.
$25.00 • Softcover • 608 pp.
978-1-891824-29-6

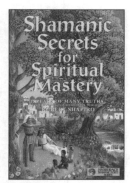

Shamanic Secrets for Spiritual Mastery
Spiritual mastery is the underpinnings of multiple ways of being, understanding, appreciating, and interacting in harmony with your world.
$29.95 • Softcover • 768 pp.
978-1-891824-58-6

THROUGH ROBERT SHAPIRO

PHONE CALLS FROM THE FUTURE

Future History & Ancient History
from the People Who Were There

Explorer Race Book 27

The channel, Robert Shapiro, and the questioner live in different cities, so the channeling sessions are conducted over the telephone.

All the beings speaking through Robert in this book live now in the future in various times and places but have had lives on Earth or visited Earth during the times they speak about for this book.

$25.00 • Softcover • 320 PP.
978-1-62233-096-6

PART ONE: FUTURE HISTORY

- Mining on the Moon
- Life on the Moon
- Future from the Moon
- Doc's Identity
- Life on the Moon
- Water on the Moon
- The Origins of the Moon
- Stop Digging Toxic Matter on Earth and Live 700 Years
- Children and Dogs on Mars

PART ONE: ANCIENT HISTORY

- Spirits of the Biloba Tree Created Yeti (Bigfoot) People
- Protection from Earth's Violence
- Earth's History of ET Visitations
- Ancient Cultures Moved Stones through Love
- Gobekli Tepe, Turkey — Ancient Pleiadian Healing and Manifestation Circles
- Dolmens: ET Gifts to Ensure Early Humans' Survival

🕊 *Light Technology* PUBLISHING *Presents*   283

TO ORDER PRINT BOOKS
Visit LightTechnology.com, Call 928-526-1345 or 1-800-450-0985,
or Check Amazon.com or Your Favorite Bookstore

BOOKS THROUGH TINA LOUISE SPALDING

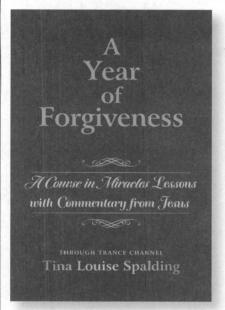

A Year of Forgiveness
A Course in Miracles Lessons with Commentary from Jesus

Keep this book close at hand with your *A Course in Miracles* manual, and read Jesus's commentaries after practicing the lesson as described in that text. Allow Jesus's simple and direct discussion of the topic to aid your understanding of these wonderful teachings.

This book is made even more appealing by the whimsical art of Renee Phillips, who has contributed beautiful illustrations for each lesson.

A Course in Miracles will change your life. With this companion book, find help and a clearer understanding of the lessons through these 365 channeled messages from Jesus.

Features hundreds of full-color illustrations by Renée Phillips

Print Pub Date: September 30, 2020
$25.00 • 496 PP. • 978-1-62233-076-8

Jesus: My Autobiography
$16.95 • Softcover • 304 PP.
978-1-62233-030-0

Love and a Map to the Unaltered Soul
$16.95 • Softcover • 240 PP.
ISBN 978-1-62233-047-8

Making Love to God: The Path to Divine Sex
$19.95 • Softcover • 416 PP.
978-1-62233-003-6

Spirit of the Western Way
$16.95 • Softcover • 176 PP.
978-1-62233-051-5

You Can Free Yourself from the Karma of Chaos
$16.95 • Softcover • 224 PP.
978-1-62233-057-5

Great Minds Speak to You
$19.95 • Softcover • 192 PP.
Includes CD
978-1-62233-010-2

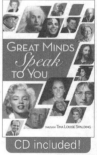

All Our Books Are Also Available as eBooks from Amazon, Apple iTunes, Google Play, Barnes & Noble, and Kobo.

THROUGH RAE CHANDRAN

PARTNER WITH ANGELS

And Benefit Every Area of Your Life

channeled by Rae Chandran
with Robert Mason Pollock

$16.95 • Softcover • 208 pp. • 978-1-62233-034-8

CHAPTERS INCLUDE
- The Benefits of Working with Angels
- Prepare for a New Consciousness
- Design Your Unique Path
- Access Support from Celestial Bodies
- Invoke Vibrational Support and Activation
- Practice Universal Communication
- Develop Environmental Connections
- You Are the New Masters

Partner with Angels and Benefit Every Area of Your Life

Angels are the Creator's workforce, and in this book, individual angels describe their responsibilities and explain how they can help you with all aspects of your life — practical and spiritual. All you need to do is ask.

Many of these angels have never spoken to human beings before or revealed their names or what they do. Here are some examples of what you will find inside:

- **La Banaha**, the essence of the Moon, explains feminine empowerment and organ rejuvenation.
- **Angel Anauel** describes fair commerce.
- **Angel Tahariel** helps you purify and shift your vibration.
- **Angel Mansu** gives advice about how to eliminate the trauma from birthing procedures.
- **Angel Agon** inspires writers and filmmakers and relates how you can call on him for inspiration.
- **Angel Tadzekiel** helps you access your wisdom and put it into perspective.
- **Archangel Maroni** downloads your individual pathway to ascension.

The purpose of this material is to bring the awareness of angels in a much more practical, easy-to-understand way. Call on the angels to show you the potential you have in your life to create a new reality.

TO ORDER PRINT BOOKS
Visit LightTechnology.com, Call 928-526-1345 or 1-800-450-0985,
or Check Amazon.com or Your Favorite Bookstore

Amiya's Encyclopedia of Healing through Cathy Chapman

Trauma and PTSD

Resolve the Pain to Recover Your Life

Amma's Healing Friends, known as Amiya, take you through a process so simple that all you need to do is read as you allow the release of all that is not you. What is not you? The pain, the horror, the fear, the rage, and even the energy of those who harmed you that are trapped within you — none of those things are who you are.

Know that you deserve complete healing, and accept that healing. You can have your life back again.

$25.00 • Softcover • 512 pp. • 978-1-62233-080-5

Reclaim Your Sexuality

How to Heal from the Words, Actions, and Beliefs That Deny Who You Are

Sexuality is integral to who you are, and when someone damages that, it damages your energy field. In this book, we will work at strengthening and healing your energy field so that you become comfortable with how you choose to express your sexuality.

We will show you how to dismantle the energies of non-acceptance for who you are. We will also discuss how your sexuality influences every part of your life.

$25.00 • Softcover • 368 pp. • 978-1-62233-082-9

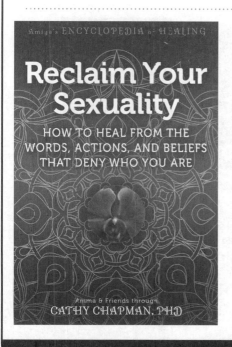

BY LYSSA ROYAL-HOLT

Galactic Heritage Cards

THE FIRST AND ONLY OF THEIR KIND:
This 108-card divination system, based
on material from Lyssa Royal-Holt's
groundbreaking book *The Prism of
Lyra*, is **designed to help you tap into
your star lineage and karmic patterns**
while revealing lessons brought to
Earth from the stars and how those
lessons can be used in your life on
Earth now. Includes a 156-page book of
instruction and additional information.

Illustrations by David Cow • 108 cards (2.75 x 4.5 inches)
156-page softcover book (4.5 x 5.5 inches) • $34.95 • 978-1-891824-88-3

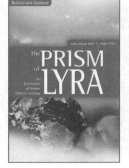

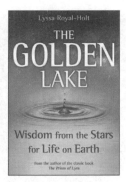

Preparing for Contact
In this book, you will take an
inner journey through your
own psyche and discover a
whole new dimension to your
unexplained experiences.
$16.95 • Softcover • 320 PP.
978-1-891824-90-6

The Prism of Lyra
This text explores the idea
that collective humanoid
consciousness created this
universe for specific purposes.
$16.95 • Softcover • 192 PP.
978-1-891824-87-6

The Golden Lake
This book features Pleiadian
and Sirian awakening teachings
that together provide a road
map for the next phase of
human evolution — the
integration of polarity
and the awakening of our
consciousness beyond duality.
$19.95 • Softcover • 240 PP.

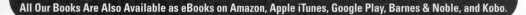

LITTLE ANGEL SERIES BY LEIA STINNETT